Sun[...]

for Young Catholics

2024-2025

I want to know Jesus better.

This missal will help you take part in the Mass on Sundays and important feast days. Pages 2 through 31 contain the words and explain the gestures that are the same for every Mass. The rest of the book gives you the Scripture readings for each Sunday of the year.

Look over the readings with your family before you go to church. This is an excellent way to use this book and a wonderful way to prepare for Mass.

The most important thing about this little book is that it will help you to know Jesus better. Jesus came to bring God's love into the world. And his Spirit continues to fill us with love for one another.

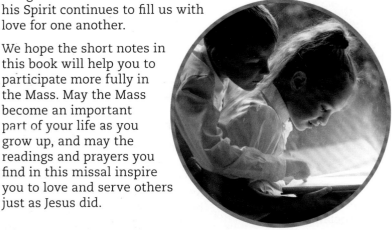

We hope the short notes in this book will help you to participate more fully in the Mass. May the Mass become an important part of your life as you grow up, and may the readings and prayers you find in this missal inspire you to love and serve others just as Jesus did.

The **altar** is the table where the priest consecrates bread and wine. The **priest** makes Jesus present and acts in his name.

A group of Christians. You are a Christian by your baptism.

One **cruet** contains water, while the other cruet contains wine.

Two **books** are used at Mass: the missal contains the prayers of the Mass, and the lectionary contains the readings.

Holy vessels

chalice   ciborium   paten

Bread and wine
The Mass is the commemoration of what Jesus did during the Last Supper with his disciples, before he died. The bread is shaped like a small disc and is called a "host."

The **ambo** is the place where the word of God is proclaimed.

On the following pages you will find the words that the priest says and the responses we say together during each part of the Mass. You will also find explanations and responses to many questions that people ask about the Mass.

The Introductory Rites

The Lord brings us together.
We ask God for forgiveness.
We give glory to God.

The Liturgy of the Word

We listen to the word of God.
We profess our faith.
We pray for the whole world.

The Liturgy of the Eucharist

We offer bread and wine to God.
We give thanks to God.
We say the Lord's Prayer.
We share the peace of Christ.
We receive Jesus in communion.

The Concluding Rites

The Lord sends us forth to live
the gospel.

The Lord Brings Us Together

We come together in church with family, friends, neighbors, and strangers. We are here because Jesus has invited us to be here.

When the priest comes in, we stand and sing. Then we make the sign of the cross along with the priest.

Priest: In the name of the Father, and of the Son,
and of the Holy Spirit.

Everyone: Amen.

Sometimes, the words can change a bit, but usually the priest will say:

Priest: The grace of our Lord Jesus Christ,
and the love of God,
and the communion of the Holy Spirit
be with you all.

Everyone: And with your spirit.

Questions

Why do we celebrate Mass on Sunday?

Jesus rose from the dead on Sunday, the day after the Sabbath. This is why Christians gather on that day. Over time, people started to call it "the Lord's day."

Why do we celebrate Mass in a church?

Churches are built specially for Christians to gather in. If needed, Mass can be celebrated in other places: a home, a school, a plaza, a jail, a hospital, a park...

Why do we need a priest to celebrate Mass?

We believe that Jesus is present in the person of the priest when Christians gather for the Mass. He presides over the celebration of the Lord's supper in the name of Jesus Christ.

Gestures

Standing

We stand to welcome Jesus, who is present among us when we gather in his name.

The sign of the cross

With our right hand we make the sign of the cross (from our forehead to our chest, from our left shoulder to our right) and say "In the name of the Father, and of the Son, and of the Holy Spirit." This is how all Catholic prayer begins.

Singing

This is a joyful way to pray together.

We Ask God for Forgiveness

We speak to God and we recognize that we have done wrong. We ask forgiveness for our misdeeds. God, who knows and loves us, forgives us.

Priest: Brothers and sisters, let us acknowledge our sins, and so prepare ourselves to celebrate the sacred mysteries.

We silently recognize our faults and allow God's loving forgiveness to touch us.

Everyone: I **confess** to almighty God
and to you, my brothers and sisters,
that I have greatly sinned,
in my thoughts and in my words,
in what I have done and in what I have failed to do,
(tap the heart) through my fault,
through my fault,
through my most grievous fault;
therefore I ask blessed Mary ever-Virgin,
all the Angels and Saints,
and you, my brothers and sisters,
to pray for me to the Lord our God.

Priest: May almighty God have **mercy** on us,
forgive us our sins,
and bring us to everlasting life.

Everyone: **Amen.**

Priest: **Lord**, have mercy.

Everyone: Lord, have mercy.

Priest: **Christ**, have mercy.

Everyone: Christ, have mercy.

Priest: Lord, have mercy.

Everyone: Lord, have mercy.

What Does It Mean?

Confess
We recognize before others that we have turned away from God, who is love.

Mercy
We know God is full of mercy—that he loves us even when we have sinned. God's mercy is always there for us.

Amen
This is a Hebrew word meaning "Yes, I agree. I commit myself."

Lord
This is a name that we give to God. Christians call Jesus "Lord" because we believe he is the Son of God.

Christ or Messiah
In the Bible, these words designate someone who has been blessed with perfumed oil. This blessing is a sign that God has given a mission to the person. Christians give this name to Jesus.

Gestures

Tapping our heart
This is a way of showing we are very sorry for our sins.

We Give Glory to God

We recognize God's greatness when we say "Glory to God." This prayer begins with the hymn the angels sang when they announced Jesus' birth to the shepherds.

Everyone:
Glory to God in the highest,
and on earth peace to people of good will.

We **praise** you,
we bless you,
we adore you,
we glorify you,
we give you thanks for your great glory,
Lord God, heavenly King,
O God, **almighty** Father.

Lord Jesus Christ, Only Begotten Son,
Lord God, Lamb of God, Son of the Father,
you take away the **sins of the world**,
    have mercy on us;
you take away the sins of the world,
    receive our prayer;
you are seated at the right hand of the Father,
    have mercy on us.

For you alone are the Holy One,
you alone are the Lord,
you alone are the Most High,
Jesus Christ,
with the **Holy Spirit**,
in the glory of God the Father.
Amen.

Priest:
Let us pray.

The priest invites us to pray. He then says a prayer in the name of all of us and finishes like this:

Through our Lord Jesus Christ, your Son, who lives and reigns with you in the unity of the Holy Spirit, God, for ever and ever.

Everyone:
Amen.

What Does It Mean?

Glory
With this word, we indicate the greatness of a person. It shows that a person is important. When we say "Glory to God" we are recognizing that God is important in our lives.

Praise
To praise is to speak well and enthusiastically of someone.

Almighty
When we say that God is almighty, we mean that nothing is impossible for God.

Sins of the world
This expression refers to all the evil that is done in the world.

Holy Spirit
This is the Spirit of God, our heavenly guide, who fills us with love for Jesus.

We Listen to the Word of God

This is the moment when we listen to several readings from the **Bible.** We welcome God who speaks to us today.

You can follow the readings in this book. Look for the Sunday that corresponds to the day's date.

The First Two Readings

*We sit down for these readings. The first reading is usually taken from the Old Testament. The second is from a letter written by an apostle to the first Christians. Between these two readings, we pray with the responsorial **Psalm**, which we do best when it is sung.*

The Gospel

*We stand and sing **Alleluia!** (except during Lent) as we prepare to listen carefully to a reading from one of the gospels.*

Priest: The Lord be with you.

Everyone: And with your spirit.

Priest: A reading from the holy **Gospel** according to N.

Everyone: Glory to you, O Lord.

We trace three small crosses with our thumb: one on our forehead, one on our lips, and another on our heart. When the reading is finished, the priest kisses the book and says:

Priest: The Gospel of the Lord.

Everyone: Praise to you, Lord Jesus Christ.

The Homily

We sit down to listen to the comments of the priest, which help us to understand and apply the word of God in our lives.

What Does It Mean?

Bible
This is the holy book of all Christians. The Old Testament tells the story of the covenant God made with the Jewish people before Jesus' time. The New Testament tells the story of the covenant God made with all people through his son, Jesus Christ.

Psalm
The Psalms are prayers that are found in the Bible. They are meant to be sung.

Alleluia!
This Hebrew word means "May God be praised and thanked."

Gospel
The word "gospel" means "good news." Jesus himself is the Good News who lives with us. The first four books of the New Testament are called "gospels." They transmit the good news to us.

Gestures

The sign of the cross that we make on our forehead, lips, and heart
This sign means that we want to make the gospel so much a part of our life that we can proclaim it to all around us with all our being.

Kissing the book of the gospels
When the priest does this, he says in a low voice: "Through the words of the Gospel may our sins be wiped away."

We Profess Our Faith

We have just listened to the word of God. To respond to it, we proclaim the **Creed**.

We stand up and profess our faith:

Everyone: I believe in one God,
the Father almighty,
maker of heaven and earth,
of all things visible and invisible.

I believe in one Lord Jesus Christ,
the Only Begotten Son of God,
born of the Father before all ages.
God from God, Light from Light,
true God from true God,
begotten, not made, consubstantial with the Father;
through him all things were made.
For us men and for our salvation
he came down from heaven,
(At the words that follow, up to and including
"and became man," all bow.)
and by the Holy Spirit was incarnate of the Virgin Mary,
and became man.

For our sake he was **crucified** under **Pontius Pilate**,
he suffered death and was buried,
and rose again on the third day
in accordance with the Scriptures.
He ascended into heaven
and is seated at the right hand of the Father.
He will come again in glory
to judge the living and the dead
and his kingdom will have no end.

I believe in the Holy Spirit, the Lord, the giver of life,
who proceeds from the Father and the Son,
who with the Father and the Son is adored and glorified,
who has spoken through the prophets.

I believe in one, holy, **catholic** and apostolic **Church**.
I confess one Baptism for the forgiveness of sins
and I look forward to the **resurrection** of the dead
and the life of the world to come. Amen.

What Does It Mean?

Creed
From the Latin verb *credo*, meaning "I believe." The Creed is the prayer that expresses our faith as Christians.

Crucified
Jesus died by crucifixion, meaning he was nailed to a cross.

Pontius Pilate
This is the name of the Roman governor who ordered that Jesus be crucified.

Catholic
In Greek, this word means "universal." The Church is open to all people in the world.

Church
The "Church" with a big C refers to the whole Christian community throughout the world. The "church" with a little c is a building where we gather to worship God.

Resurrection
This means coming back to life after having died. God raised Jesus from the dead and gave him new life for ever. Jesus shares that life with us.

We Pray for the Whole World

This is the moment of the Universal Prayer of the Faithful when we present our **petitions** to God. We pray for the Church, for all of humanity, for those who are sick or lonely, for children who are abandoned, for those who suffer through natural disasters...

After each petition we respond with a phrase, such as:

Everyone: Lord, hear our prayer.

Reader: For the needs of the Church...

For peace in every country...

For the hungry and the homeless...

For ourselves and for all God's children...

What Does It Mean?

Petitions
Petitions are prayers asking for something specific. Each week at Mass, the petitions change because the needs of the world and our community change. We stand for the petitions and answer "Amen" at the end. Sometimes we call these prayers intentions.

Why do we call the Prayer of the Faithful "universal"?
It is a universal prayer because it includes everyone: we pray for all the people of the world.

Why do we take up a collection?
Christians help out with the maintenance of the church building and also help people who are in need. These gifts are brought to the altar with the bread and the wine.

We Offer Bread and Wine to God

The celebration of the Lord's Supper continues at the altar. Members of the community bring the bread, the wine, and the gifts collected to relieve the needs of the Church and the poor. The priest receives the gifts and then with him we bless God for the bread and wine that will become the Body and Blood of Jesus.

We sit down. The priest takes the bread and wine, and lifts them up, saying:

Priest: **Blessed** are you, Lord God of all creation, for through your goodness we have received the bread we offer you: fruit of the earth and work of human hands, it will become for us the bread of life.

Everyone: Blessed be God for ever.

Priest: Blessed are you, Lord God of all creation, for through your goodness we have received the wine we offer you: fruit of the vine and work of human hands, it will become our spiritual drink.

Everyone: Blessed be God for ever.

The priest washes his hands. Then we all stand and the priest says:

Priest: Pray, brothers and sisters, that my sacrifice and yours may be acceptable to God, the almighty Father.

Everyone: May the Lord accept the **sacrifice** at your hands for the praise and glory of his name, for our good, and the good of all his holy Church.

The priest, with hands extended, says a prayer over the bread and wine. He usually ends the prayer by saying:

Priest: Through Christ our Lord.

Everyone: Amen.

What Does It Mean?

Eucharist
A Greek word that means "gratefulness, thanksgiving." The Mass is also called the Eucharist.

Blessed
To bless means to speak well of someone. To bless God is to give thanks for everything God gives us.

Sacrifice
God does not ask for animal sacrifice, as in the old days written about in the Bible. Nor does God ask us to die on a cross, like Jesus did. Instead, God asks us to offer our daily life, with Jesus, as a beautiful gift.

Gestures

Procession with the bread and the wine
With this gesture we present to God the fruit of our work and we give thanks for the gift of life that comes from God.

Drops of water in the wine
With this sign, the priest prays that our life be united with God's life.

Washing of hands
Before saying the most important prayer of the Mass, the priest washes his hands and asks God to wash away his sins.

We Give Thanks to God

At this moment we give thanks to God for his Son, Jesus Christ, for life, and for all that he gives us. This is how the great Eucharistic Prayer begins.

Priest: The Lord be with you.

Everyone: And with your spirit.

Priest: Lift up your hearts.

Everyone: We lift them up to the Lord.

Priest: Let us give thanks to the Lord our God.

Everyone: It is right and just.

Here is one way of celebrating the Eucharist with young Catholics. On page 21, you will find Eucharistic Prayer II, which is a common way of celebrating the Eucharist with grown-ups.

Eucharistic Prayer for Masses with Children I

Priest: God our Father,
you have brought us here together
so that we can give you thanks and praise
for all the wonderful things you have done.

We thank you for all that is beautiful in the world
and for the happiness you have given us.
We praise you for daylight
and for your word which lights up our minds.
We praise you for the earth,
and all the people who live on it,
and for our life which comes from you.

We know that you are good.
You love us and do great things for us.

So we all sing together:

Everyone: Holy, Holy, Holy Lord God of hosts.
Heaven and earth are full of your glory.
Hosanna in the highest.

Priest: Father,
you are always thinking about your people;
you never forget us.
You sent us your Son Jesus,
who gave his life for us
and who came to save us.
He cured sick people;
he cared for those who were poor
and wept with those who were sad.
He forgave sinners
and taught us to forgive each other.
He loved everyone
and showed us how to be kind.
He took children in his arms and blessed them.

So we are glad to sing:

Everyone: Blessed is he who comes in the name of the Lord.
Hosanna in the highest.

Priest: God our Father,
all over the world your people praise you.
So now we pray with the whole Church:
with N., our Pope and N., our Bishop.
In heaven the Blessed Virgin Mary,
the Apostles and all the Saints
always sing your praise.
Now we join with them and with the Angels
to adore you as we sing:

Everyone: Holy, Holy, Holy Lord God of hosts.
Heaven and earth are full of your glory.
Hosanna in the highest.
Blessed is he who comes in the name of the Lord.
Hosanna in the highest.

Priest: God our Father,
you are most holy
and we want to show you that we are grateful.
We bring you bread and wine
and ask you to send your Holy Spirit
    to make these gifts
the Body and Blood of Jesus your Son.
Then we can offer to you
what you have given to us.

On the night before he died,
Jesus was having supper with his Apostles.
He took bread from the table.
He gave you thanks and praise.
Then he broke the bread,
gave it to his friends, and said:

> TAKE THIS, ALL OF YOU, AND EAT OF IT,
> FOR THIS IS MY BODY
> WHICH WILL BE GIVEN UP FOR YOU.

When supper was ended,
Jesus took the chalice that was filled with wine.
He thanked you, gave it to his friends, and said:

> TAKE THIS, ALL OF YOU, AND DRINK FROM IT,
> FOR THIS IS THE CHALICE OF MY BLOOD,
> THE BLOOD OF THE NEW AND ETERNAL **COVENANT**,
> WHICH WILL BE POURED OUT FOR YOU AND FOR MANY
> FOR THE **FORGIVENESS OF SINS**.

Then he said to them:

> **DO THIS IN MEMORY OF ME**.

We do now what Jesus told us to do.
We remember his Death
and his Resurrection
and we offer you, Father,
the bread that gives us life,
and the chalice that saves us.
Jesus brings us to you;
welcome us as you welcome him.

Let us proclaim our faith:

Everyone: We proclaim your Death, O Lord,
and profess your Resurrection
until you come again.

Or

When we eat this Bread and drink this Cup,
we proclaim your Death, O Lord,
until you come again.

Or

Save us, Savior of the world,
for by your Cross and Resurrection
you have set us free.

Priest: Father,
because you love us,
you invite us to come to your table.
Fill us with the joy of the Holy Spirit
as we receive the Body and Blood of your Son.

Lord,
you never forget any of your children.
We ask you to take care of those we love,
especially of N. and N.,
and we pray for those who have died.
Remember everyone who is suffering
    from pain or sorrow.

Remember Christians everywhere
and all other people in the world.

We are filled with wonder and praise
when we see what you do for us
through Jesus your Son,
and so we give you praise.

Through him, and with him, and in him,
O God, almighty Father,
in the unity of the Holy Spirit,
all glory and honor is yours,
for ever and ever.

Everyone: Amen.

(Turn to page 25)

Eucharistic Prayer II

Priest: It is truly right and just, our duty and our salvation,
always and everywhere to give you thanks,
    Father most holy,
through your beloved Son, Jesus Christ,
your Word through whom you made all things,
whom you sent as our Savior and Redeemer,
incarnate by the Holy Spirit and born of the Virgin.

Fulfilling your will and gaining for you a holy people,
he stretched out his hands
as he endured his Passion,
so as to break the bonds of death and manifest
    the resurrection.

And so, with the Angels and all the Saints
we declare your glory,
as with one voice we acclaim:

Everyone: Holy, Holy, Holy Lord God of hosts.
Heaven and earth are full of your glory.
Hosanna in the highest.
Blessed is he who comes in the name of the Lord.
Hosanna in the highest.

Priest: You are indeed Holy, O Lord,
the fount of all holiness.

Make holy, therefore, these gifts, we pray,
by sending down your Spirit upon them
    like the dewfall,
so that they may become for us
the Body and Blood of our Lord Jesus Christ.

At the time he was betrayed
and entered willingly into his Passion,
he took bread and, giving thanks, broke it,
and gave it to his disciples, saying:

TAKE THIS, ALL OF YOU, AND EAT OF IT,
FOR THIS IS MY BODY
WHICH WILL BE GIVEN UP FOR YOU.

In a similar way,
when supper was ended,
he took the chalice
and, once more giving thanks,
he gave it to his disciples, saying:

TAKE THIS, ALL OF YOU, AND DRINK FROM IT,
FOR THIS IS THE CHALICE OF MY BLOOD,
THE BLOOD OF THE NEW AND ETERNAL **COVENANT**,
WHICH WILL BE POURED OUT FOR YOU AND FOR MANY
FOR THE **FORGIVENESS OF SINS**.

DO THIS IN MEMORY OF ME.

The mystery of faith.

Everyone: We proclaim your Death, O Lord,
and profess your Resurrection
until you come again.

or

When we eat this Bread and drink this Cup,
we proclaim your Death, O Lord,
until you come again.

or

Save us, Savior of the world,
for by your Cross and Resurrection
you have set us free.

Priest: Therefore, as we celebrate
the **memorial** of his Death and Resurrection,
we offer you, Lord,
the Bread of life and the Chalice of salvation,
giving thanks that you have held us worthy
to be in your presence and minister to you.

Humbly we pray
that, partaking of the Body and Blood of Christ,
we may be gathered into one by the Holy Spirit.
Remember, Lord, your Church,
spread throughout the world,
and bring her to the fullness of charity,
together with N. our Pope and N. our Bishop
and all the clergy.

Remember also our brothers and sisters
who have fallen asleep in the hope of the resurrection,
and all who have died in your mercy:
welcome them into the light of your face.
Have mercy on us all, we pray,
that with the Blessed Virgin Mary, Mother of God,
with blessed Joseph, her Spouse,
with the blessed Apostles, and all the Saints
who have pleased you throughout the ages,
we may merit to be co-heirs to **eternal life**,
and may praise and glorify you
through your Son, Jesus Christ.

Through him, and with him, and in him,
O God, almighty Father,
in the unity of the Holy Spirit,
all glory and honor is yours,
for ever and ever.

Everyone: Amen.

Gestures

Extending the hands
When the priest extends
his hands, he calls upon the
Holy Spirit to consecrate the
bread and wine, so that they
become for us the Body and
Blood of Christ.

Raising the bread
The priest lifts the
consecrated bread and then
the chalice, so that the
community may see and
respectfully adore the Body
and Blood of Christ.

Kneeling
This is a common way to
show respect and to worship.

What Does It Mean?

Covenant
When two people enter into a covenant, they promise to be faithful to one another. God entered into a covenant with us. He is our God and we are his people.

Forgiveness of sins
This is the forgiveness that comes from God, whose love is greater than our sins.

Do this in memory of me
Jesus asked the disciples to remember him by reliving what he said and did during the Last Supper.

The mystery of faith
Together we proclaim our belief in Christ who was born and died for us, rose to life, and will return one day.

Memorial
Memorial means to remember. When we remember at Mass, we're not just thinking about something that happened a long time ago. To remember Jesus' death and resurrection at Mass means that those events are real and happening now, in our celebration, in our hearts. It doesn't mean that Jesus is repeating his passion, death, and resurrection for us at each Mass, but that, at each Mass, the Holy Spirit makes the powerful saving mystery of Jesus' death and resurrection present to us. No one can explain this or fully understand it. It is part of the mystery of faith.

We may be gathered into one by the Holy Spirit
In the Mass, the Holy Spirit draws us into unity—communion—not only with Jesus, but with all the members of his Body—with the pope and our bishop and all the bishops and clergy, with every member of the Church throughout the world, with all members of the Body of Christ who share in eternal life, including the Blessed Virgin Mary, the apostles, and all the saints. When we gather at Mass, even though we can't see them, we know in faith that the whole Body of Christ is with us praising and worshiping God.

Eternal life
This is life with God, which will be given to us fully after death.

We Say the Lord's Prayer

Jesus has taught us that God is the Father of all human beings and that we can call upon God at any time. Together we recite or sing this prayer. To help us to be truly ready to receive Jesus in Communion, we need to ask for forgiveness and to forgive those who have hurt us.

Priest: At the **Savior's** command
and formed by divine teaching,
we dare to say:

Everyone: Our Father,
who art in **heaven**,
hallowed be thy name;
thy kingdom come,
thy will be done
on earth as it is in heaven.
Give us this day our daily bread,
and forgive us our **trespasses**,
as we forgive those who trespass against us;
and lead us not into **temptation**,
but deliver us from evil.

Priest: Deliver us, Lord, we pray, from every evil,
graciously grant peace in our days,
that, by the help of your mercy,
we may be always free from sin
and safe from all distress,
as we await the blessed hope
and the coming of our Savior, Jesus Christ.

Everyone: For the **kingdom**,
the power and the glory are yours
now and for ever.

What Does It Mean?

Savior
This is one of the names we give to Jesus because he saves us from evil and death.

Heaven
Heaven is a special way of being with God after our life on earth is over.

Trespasses
These refer to our lack of love and to the sins we commit.

Temptation
This is a desire we sometimes feel to do things we know are wrong.

Kingdom
Jesus speaks of God as king when he says: "The kingdom of God is at hand." With his life, Jesus shows us that God is present in our midst as a king who loves us. When we live as Jesus did, we welcome the kingdom of God.

gwithchrist.us

We Share the Peace of Christ

God is our Father and we are brothers and sisters in Christ. In order to show that we are one family, the priest invites us to offer each other a sign of peace.

Priest: Lord Jesus Christ,
who said to your Apostles:
Peace I leave you, my peace I give you,
look not on our sins,
but on the faith of your Church,
and graciously grant her peace and **unity**
in accordance with your will.
Who live and reign for ever and ever.

Everyone: Amen.

Priest: The peace of the Lord be with you always.

Everyone: And with your spirit.

Priest: Let us offer each other the sign of peace.

At this time, by a handshake, a hug, or a bow, we give to those near us a sign of Christ's peace. Immediately after, we sing or say:

Everyone: **Lamb of God**, you take away the sins of the world, have mercy on us.

Lamb of God, you take away the sins of the world, have mercy on us.

Lamb of God, you take away the sins of the world, grant us peace.

What Does It Mean?

Unity
When we get together each Sunday to celebrate the Lord's Supper, we recognize our unity, or oneness, since we are all children of the same loving Father.

Lamb of God
In the Old Testament, believers offered a lamb to God. We call Jesus the Lamb of God because he offers his life to God.

Gestures

The Sign of Peace
We shake hands, hug, or bow to one another to share the peace that comes from Christ. It is a sign of our commitment to live in peace with others.

We Receive Jesus in Communion

When we receive communion, the Bread of Life, Jesus feeds us with his very self.

The priest breaks the host and says:

Priest: Behold the Lamb of God,
behold him who takes away the sins of the world.
Blessed are those called to the supper of the Lamb.

Everyone: Lord, I am not worthy
that you should enter under my roof,
but only say the word
and my soul shall be healed.

It is time to come up to receive communion. The priest or the communion minister says:

Priest: The Body of Christ.

Everyone: Amen.

livingwithchrist.us

Questions

Why do we go to communion?
When we eat the bread, we receive Jesus. He gives himself to us this way so we can live for God. Sharing the Body and Blood of Christ in communion creates among us a special "one-ness" with God and with each other.

Why is the bread we share during Mass called a "host"?
The word "host" means "victim who is offered." The consecrated host is Jesus Christ, who offers himself in order to give life to others.

Gestures

The priest breaks the bread
The priest breaks the bread in the same way that Jesus did during the Last Supper, in order to share it. The early Christians used to call the Mass "the breaking of the bread."

Receiving the host
The priest or communion minister places the host in your open left hand. You pick the host up with your right hand, put the host in your mouth, eat the bread carefully, and return to your place. You take a few moments of quiet prayer to thank God for this Bread of Life.

rist.us

The Lord Sends Us Forth

After announcements, the priest blesses us in the name of God. We are then sent to live out our faith among all the people we meet during the week.

Priest: The Lord be with you.

Everyone: And with your spirit.

Priest: May almighty God bless you,
the Father, and the Son, and the Holy Spirit.

Everyone: Amen.

Then the priest sends us out, saying this or something similar:

Priest: Go in peace, glorifying the Lord by your life.

Everyone: Thanks be to God.

ithchrist.us

What Does It Mean?

The word "Mass"

The word "Mass" comes from the second word in the Latin phrase that was once used by the priest to announce the end of the Sunday celebration: *Ite missa est*—Go forth, the Mass is ended.

Communion for the sick

Sometimes people who are sick cannot be present at Sunday Mass. Certain members of the parish, known as communion ministers, can take consecrated hosts to the homes of sick people so that they can receive communion and be assured that the rest of the community is praying for them.

Gestures

Blessing

The priest makes the sign of the cross over the people in church. With this blessing we are sent out with the loving strength of God to live a life of love and service to others.

Dismissal

We cannot stay together in the church all week. When the Mass is ended, we must go our separate ways, in peace and love, to witness to the risen Jesus in the world today.

December 1

1st Sunday of Advent

First Reading (Jeremiah 33:14-16)

The days are coming, says the LORD, when I will fulfill the promise I made to the **house of Israel and Judah**. In those days, in that time, I will raise up for David a just **shoot**; he shall do what is right and just in the land. In those days Judah shall be safe and Jerusalem shall dwell secure; this is what they shall call her: "The LORD our justice."

The word of the Lord. **Thanks be to God.**

Responsorial Psalm (Psalm 25:4-5, 8-9, 10, 14)

R. **To you, O Lord, I lift my soul.**

Your ways, O LORD, make known to me;
 teach me your paths,
guide me in your truth and teach me,
 for you are God my savior,
 and for you I wait all the day. R.

Good and upright is the LORD;
 thus he shows sinners the way.
He guides the humble to justice,
 and teaches the humble his way. R.

All the paths of the LORD are kindness and constancy
 toward those who keep his covenant and his decrees.
The friendship of the LORD is with those who fear him,
 and his covenant, for their instruction. R.

Second Reading (1 Thessalonians 3:12–4:2)

Brothers and sisters: May the Lord make you increase and abound in love for one another and for all, just as we have for you, so as to strengthen your hearts, to be blameless in holiness before our God and Father at the coming of our Lord Jesus with all his holy ones. Amen.

Finally, brothers and sisters, we earnestly ask and exhort you in the Lord Jesus that, as you received from us how you should conduct yourselves to please God—and as you are conducting yourselves—you do so even more. For you know what instructions we gave you through the Lord Jesus.

The word of the Lord. **Thanks be to God.**

Gospel (Luke 21:25-28, 34-36)

A reading from the holy Gospel according to Luke.
Glory to you, O Lord.

Jesus said to his disciples: "There will be signs in the sun, the moon, and the stars, and on earth nations will be in dismay, perplexed by the roaring of the sea and the waves. People will die of fright in anticipation of what is coming upon the world, for the powers of the heavens will be shaken. And then they will see the Son of Man coming in a cloud with power and great glory. But when these signs begin to happen, stand erect and raise your heads because your redemption is at hand.

"Beware that your hearts do not become drowsy from carousing and drunkenness and the anxieties of daily life, and that day catch you by surprise like a trap. For that day will assault everyone who lives on the face of the earth. **Be vigilant** at all times and pray that you have the strength to escape the tribulations that are imminent and to stand before the Son of Man."

The Gospel of the Lord. **Praise to you, Lord Jesus Christ**

Key Words

With the season of **Advent,** which means "coming," we begin a new liturgical year. Advent lasts four weeks and during this time the liturgical color is violet or purple. Purple is the color of waiting; it reminds us to prepare our hearts to celebrate the birth of Jesus at Christmas and his return at the end of time.

Jeremiah lived about 600 years before Jesus. When Jeremiah was still a young boy, God called him to guide the people of Israel back to God. Many people ignored Jeremiah at first and sent him away. But when the people of Israel feared that God had stopped loving them, Jeremiah gave them hope that God would not abandon them.

At the time of Jeremiah, God's people were divided into two kingdoms: the **house of Israel** in the north and the **house of Judah** in the south. Jeremiah announced God's wish for both kingdoms to be united into one nation under one covenant.

A **Branch** for David is the family that is descended from David: his children and all who are born from them. When the prophet Jeremiah announced a new branch, he was speaking of the coming of the Messiah, the Christ.

Paul wrote two letters to the **Thessalonians,** Christians who lived in Thessalonica in Greece. In this letter Paul praises them and encourages them to continue to love one another.

Jesus tells his friends to **be alert** at all times, ready to meet the Son of Man whenever he arrives. Advent is a time of waiting, and we too are called to be alert for the coming of Jesus into our lives.

December 8

2nd Sunday of Advent

First Reading (Baruch 5:1-9)

Jerusalem, take off your robe of mourning and misery;
put on the splendor of glory from God forever:
wrapped in the cloak of justice from God,
    bear on your head the mitre
    that displays the glory of the eternal name.
For God will show all the earth your splendor:
    you will be named by God forever
    the peace of justice, the glory of God's worship.

Up, Jerusalem! stand upon the heights;
    look to the east and see your children
gathered from the **east and the west**
    at the word of the Holy One,
    rejoicing that they are remembered by God.
Led away on foot by their enemies they left you:
    but God will bring them back to you
    borne aloft in glory as on royal thrones.
For God has commanded
    that every lofty mountain be made low,
and that the age-old depths and gorges
    be filled to level ground,
    that Israel may advance secure in the glory of God.
The forests and every fragrant kind of tree
    have overshadowed Israel at God's command;
for God is leading Israel in joy
    by the light of his glory,
    with his mercy and justice for company.

The word of the Lord. **Thanks be to God.**

Responsorial Psalm (Psalm 126:1-2, 2-3, 4-5, 6)

R. **The Lord has done great things for us;
we are filled with joy.**

When the LORD brought back the captives of Zion,
    we were like men dreaming.
Then our mouth was filled with laughter,
    and our tongue with rejoicing. R.

Then they said among the nations,
    "The LORD has done great things for them."
The LORD has done great things for us;
    we are glad indeed. R.

Restore our fortunes, O LORD,
    like the torrents in the southern desert.
Those who sow in tears
    shall reap rejoicing. R.

Although they go forth weeping,
    carrying the seed to be sown,
they shall come back rejoicing,
    carrying their sheaves. R.

Second Reading (Philippians 1:4-6, 8-11)

Brothers and sisters: I pray always with joy in my every prayer for all of you, because of your partnership for the gospel from the first day until now. I am confident of this, that the one who began a good work in you will continue to complete it until the day of Christ Jesus. God is my witness, how I long for all of you with the affection of Christ Jesus. And this is my prayer: that your love may increase ever more and more in **knowledge and every kind of perception**, to discern what is of value, so that you may be pure and blameless for the day of Christ, filled with the fruit of righteousness that comes through Jesus Christ for the glory and praise of God.

The word of the Lord. **Thanks be to God.**

Gospel (Luke 3:1-6)

A reading from the holy Gospel according to Luke.
Glory to you, O Lord.

In the fifteenth year of the reign of **Tiberius Caesar**, when **Pontius Pilate** was governor of Judea, and **Herod** was tetrarch* of Galilee, and his brother Philip tetrarch of the region of Ituraea* and Trachonitis,* and Lysanias* was tetrarch of Abilene, during the high priesthood of Annas and Caiaphas,* the word of God came to John the son of Zechariah* in the desert. John went throughout the whole region of the Jordan, proclaiming a **baptism of repentance** for the forgiveness of sins, as it is written in the book of the words of the prophet Isaiah:

> A voice of one crying out in the desert:
> "Prepare the way of the Lord,
>   make straight his paths.
> Every valley shall be filled
>   and every mountain and hill shall be made low.
> The winding roads shall be made straight,
>   and the rough ways made smooth,
> and all flesh shall see the salvation of God."

The Gospel of the Lord. **Praise to you, Lord Jesus Christ.**

Key Words

The **book of the Prophet Baruch** was written about 200 years before Jesus was born. It tells the story of the people of Israel while they were forced to live in exile in Babylon. Baruch urges the people to follow God and stay faithful to him.

From **west and east** means from all across the world — similar to saying "from all the corners of the world." This statement reminds us that God desires all people to live in peace.

When he was in prison, Paul wrote a letter to the **Philippians,** a community of Christians in Philippi, Greece. He thanked them for their help and encouraged them to keep their faith in Jesus strong.

Knowledge and full insight are gifts from God. They help us to know what God wants us to do.

Emperor Tiberius was a Roman emperor who ruled after Augustus Caesar. He ruled the Roman Empire during the time Jesus lived.

Pontius Pilate was appointed by the Romans to govern the area of Judea, the southern region of Israel. Jerusalem and Bethlehem were located in Judea.

Herod was the Jewish ruler of Galilee, an area in the south of Israel, during the time of the Emperor Tiberius. Nazareth was located in Galilee; this is why Jesus was called a Galilean. The Herod mentioned in today's Gospel was the son of King Herod who ruled at the time of Jesus' birth.

A **baptism of repentance** is a sign that a person wants to turn back to God. John the Baptist baptized people in the River Jordan to show that their sins were washed away. Today, the sacrament of baptism unites us with Jesus and makes us part of the Church.

40

livingwithchrist.us

December 9
The Immaculate Conception
of the Blessed Virgin Mary

First Reading (Genesis 3:9-15, 20)

After the man, **Adam**, had eaten of the tree, the Lord God called to the man and asked him, "Where are you?" He answered, "I heard you in the garden; but I was afraid, because I was naked, so I hid myself." Then he asked, "Who told you that you were naked? You have eaten, then, from the tree of which I had forbidden you to eat!" The man replied, "The woman whom you put here with me—she gave me fruit from the tree, and so I ate it." The Lord God then asked the woman, "Why did you do such a thing?" The woman answered, "The serpent tricked me into it, so I ate it."

Then the Lord God said to the serpent:
"Because you have done this, you shall be banned
from all the animals
and from all the wild creatures;
on your belly shall you crawl,
and dirt shall you eat
all the days of your life.
I will put enmity between you and the woman,
and between your offspring and hers;
he will strike at your head,
while you strike at his heel."

The man called his wife **Eve**, because she became the mother of all the living.

The word of the Lord. **Thanks be to God.**

Responsorial Psalm (Psalm 98:1, 2-3ab, 3cd-4)

R. **Sing to the Lord a new song,
for he has done marvelous deeds.**

Sing to the Lord a new song,
for he has done wondrous deeds;
His right hand has won victory for him,
his holy arm. R.

The LORD has made his salvation known:
in the sight of the nations he has revealed his justice.
He has remembered his kindness and his faithfulness
toward the house of Israel. ℟.

All the ends of the earth have seen
the salvation by our God.
Sing joyfully to the LORD, all you lands;
break into song; sing praise. ℟.

Second Reading (Ephesians 1:3-6, 11-12)

Brothers and sisters: Blessed be the God and Father of our Lord Jesus Christ, who has blessed us in Christ with every spiritual blessing in the heavens, as he chose us in him, before the foundation of the world, to be holy and without blemish before him. In love he destined us for **adoption** to himself through Jesus Christ, in accord with the favor of his will, for the praise of the glory of his grace that he granted us in the beloved.

In him we were also chosen, destined in accord with the purpose of the One who accomplishes all things according to the intention of his will, so that we might exist for the praise of his glory, we who first hoped in Christ.

The word of the Lord. **Thanks be to God.**

Gospel (Luke 1:26-38)

A reading from the holy Gospel according to Luke.
Glory to you, O Lord.

The angel Gabriel was sent from God to a town of Galilee called Nazareth, to a virgin betrothed to a man named Joseph, of the house of David, and the virgin's name was Mary. And coming to her, he said, "Hail, full of grace! The Lord is with you." But she was greatly troubled at what was said and pondered what sort of greeting this might be. Then the angel said to her, "Do not be afraid, Mary, for you have found favor with God. Behold, you will conceive in your womb and bear a son, and you shall name him Jesus. He will be great and will be called Son of the Most High, and the Lord God will give him the throne of David his father, and he will rule over the house of Jacob forever, and of his Kingdom there will be no end." But Mary said to the angel, "How can this be, since I have no relations with a man?" And the angel said to her in reply, "The Holy Spirit will come upon you, and the power of the Most High will overshadow you. Therefore the child to be born will be called holy, the Son of God. And behold, Elizabeth, your relative, has also conceived a son in her old age, and this is the sixth month for her who was called barren; for nothing will be impossible for God." Mary said, "Behold, I am the handmaid of the Lord. May it be done to me according to your word." Then the angel departed from her.

The Gospel of the Lord. **Praise to you, Lord Jesus Christ.**

Key Words

The **Immaculate Conception** is the day we remember that God kept the Virgin Mary free from sin from the very beginning of her life. God did this for Mary because she was the mother of our Savior, Jesus, and it is through Jesus that all of us, including Mary, are redeemed and saved from sin.

Some stories are true on the inside, even if they are not completely true on the outside. The Church does not teach that the story of **Adam** and **Eve** happened just as it is told in this reading. But it does teach that this story tells us a very important truth about how human beings first turned away from God—and often still do. When God says **"he will strike at your head,"** the Church believes that God is speaking about Jesus, who will come and save human beings from sin.

Children without parents can be adopted into new families. A similar process of **adoption** happened in our baptism. Through baptism, we have been adopted by God, our heavenly parent. We have become brothers and sisters of Jesus, brothers and sisters to one another, all of us children of God, called to share God's love and life.

December 15

3rd Sunday of Advent

First Reading (Zephaniah 3:14-18a)

Shout for joy, O **daughter Zion**!
    Sing joyfully, O Israel!
Be glad and exult with all your heart,
    O daughter Jerusalem!
The LORD has removed the judgment against you;
    he has turned away your enemies;
the King of Israel, the LORD, is in your midst,
    you have no further misfortune to fear.
On that day, it shall be said to Jerusalem:
    Fear not, O Zion, be not discouraged!
The LORD, your God, is in your midst,
    a mighty savior;
he will **rejoice** over you with gladness,
    and renew you in his love,
he will sing joyfully because of you,
    as one sings at festivals.

The word of the Lord. **Thanks be to God.**

Responsorial Psalm (Isaiah 12:2-3, 4, 5-6)

R. **Cry out with joy and gladness: for among you is the great and Holy One of Israel.**

God indeed is my savior;
    I am confident and unafraid.
My strength and my courage is the LORD,
    and he has been my savior.
With joy you will draw water
    at the fountain of salvation. R.

Give thanks to the LORD, acclaim his name;
    among the nations make known his deeds,
    proclaim how exalted is his name. R.

Sing praise to the LORD for his glorious achievement;
    let this be known throughout all the earth.
Shout with exultation, O city of Zion,
    for great in your midst
    is the Holy One of Israel! R.

Second Reading (Philippians 4:4-7)

Brothers and sisters: Rejoice in the Lord always. I shall say it again: rejoice! Your kindness should be known to all. The Lord is near. Have no anxiety at all, but in everything, by prayer and petition, with thanksgiving, make your requests known to God. Then the peace of God that surpasses all understanding will guard your hearts and minds in Christ Jesus.

The word of the Lord. **Thanks be to God.**

Gospel (Luke 3:10-18)

A reading from the holy Gospel according to Luke.
Glory to you, O Lord.

The crowds asked John the Baptist, "What should we do?" He said to them in reply, "Whoever has two cloaks should share with the person who has none. And whoever has food should do likewise." Even **tax collectors** came to be baptized and they said to him, "Teacher, what should we do?" He answered them, "Stop collecting more than what is prescribed." Soldiers also asked him, "And what is it that we should do?" He told them, "Do not practice **extortion**, do not falsely accuse anyone, and be satisfied with your wages."

Now the people were filled with expectation, and all were asking in their hearts whether John might be the Christ. John answered them all, saying, "I am baptizing you with water, but one mightier than I is coming. I am not worthy to loosen the thongs of his sandals. He will baptize you with the Holy Spirit and fire. His **winnowing fan** is in his hand to clear his threshing floor and to gather the wheat into his barn, but the chaff he will burn with unquenchable fire." Exhorting them in many other ways, he preached good news to the people.

The Gospel of the Lord. **Praise to you, Lord Jesus Christ.**

Key Words

The prophet **Zephaniah** lived about 700 years before Jesus was born. The people of Israel had fallen away from their faith. Zephaniah tried to help them find their way back to God.

Zion is the name of a hill in Jerusalem where the temple was built, but the city itself was often called Zion. **Daughter Zion** is another way of naming the entire nation, the whole people of God.

The Third Sunday of Advent is called "Gaudete" Sunday: gaudete (pronounced gow-day-tay) is a Latin word for **"Rejoice!"** In today's readings, the Prophet Zephaniah, the Psalmist and Saint Paul all tell us to rejoice. Saint Paul tells the Philippians to rejoice and be happy because we all live in the Lord. Nothing can separate us from God's love.

The Jewish people didn't like **tax collectors** because they worked for the Romans, who were foreigners ruling over Israel. Also, many tax collectors cheated people and took more money for taxes than they were supposed to.

To **extort** money is to force people to give money against their will. Jesus tells us always to be honest with others and treat everyone fairly.

A **winnowing fork** is a big wooden tool for separating the wheat, which is good to eat, from its husk, which is not edible. It separates the good from the bad.

December 22

4th Sunday of Advent

First Reading (Micah 5:1-4a)

Thus says the LORD:
You, **Bethlehem**-Ephrathah,
    too small to be among the clans of Judah,
from you shall come forth for me
    one who is to be ruler in Israel;
whose origin is from of old,
    from ancient times.
Therefore the Lord will give them up, until the time
    when she who is to give birth has borne,
and the rest of his kindred shall return
    to the children of Israel.
He shall stand firm and shepherd his flock
    by the strength of the LORD,
    in the majestic name of the LORD, his God;
and they shall remain, for now his greatness
    shall reach to the ends of the earth;
    he shall be peace.

The word of the Lord. **Thanks be to God.**

Responsorial Psalm (Psalm 80:2-3, 15-16, 18-19)

R. **Lord, make us turn to you; let us see your face and we shall be saved.**

O shepherd of Israel, hearken,
    from your throne upon the cherubim,* shine forth.
Rouse your power,
    and come to save us. R.

Once again, O LORD of hosts,
    look down from heaven, and see;
take care of this vine,
    and protect what your right hand has planted,
the son of man whom you yourself made strong. R.

May your help be with the man of your right hand,
    with the son of man whom you yourself made strong.
Then we will no more withdraw from you;
    give us new life, and we will call upon your name. R.

Second Reading (Hebrews 10:5-10)

Brothers and sisters: When Christ came into the world, he said:

"Sacrifice and offering you did not desire,
   but a body you prepared for me;
in holocausts and sin offerings you took no delight.
Then I said, 'As is written of me in the scroll,
behold, I come to do your will, O God.' "

First he says, "Sacrifices and offerings, holocausts and sin offerings, you neither desired nor delighted in." These are offered according to the law. Then he says, "Behold, I come to do **your will**." He takes away the first to establish the second. By this "will," we have been consecrated through the offering of the body of Jesus Christ once for all.

The word of the Lord. **Thanks be to God.**

Gospel (Luke 1:39-45)

A reading from the holy Gospel according to Luke.
Glory to you, O Lord.

Mary set out and traveled to the hill country in haste to a town of Judah, where she entered the house of Zechariah and greeted **Elizabeth**. When Elizabeth heard Mary's greeting, the infant leaped in her womb, and Elizabeth, filled with the Holy Spirit, cried out in a loud voice and said, "**Blessed are you among women**, and blessed is the fruit of your womb. And how does this happen to me, that the mother of my Lord should come to me? For at the moment the sound of your greeting reached my ears, the infant in my womb leaped for joy. Blessed are you who believed that what was spoken to you by the Lord would be fulfilled."

The Gospel of the Lord. **Praise to you, Lord Jesus Christ.**

Key Words

Micah was a prophet who lived about 700 years before Jesus was born. It was a hard time for Israel. The Assyrians were taking over and the Israelites were not working together or helping the poor. Micah told the people God was angry with them, but there was hope: if they changed their ways, things would get better.

Bethlehem is the city of King David, one of Jesus' ancestors. It is south of Jerusalem in Judea. Jesus was born there.

Jesus came to do **God's will:** what God wanted him to do or make happen. When we pray the Our Father, we say to God, "Thy will be done." God's will was to save us from sin and bring us peace through Jesus. We are also to do God's will: to help build his kingdom of peace.

Mary was an ordinary person who was asked to do an extraordinary thing. God asked Mary, who was engaged to be married to Joseph, to be the mother of God's son, Jesus. She said yes. We are thankful for Mary's generosity because, through her son, Jesus, we have eternal life. Since Jesus is our brother, Mary is also our mother. She listens to our prayers and presents them to Jesus for us.

Elizabeth, Mary's cousin, became pregnant at an age when women can no longer have children. Her husband, Zechariah, was a priest of the temple in Jerusalem. Their son, John the Baptist, Jesus' cousin, was six months older than Jesus.

Blessed are you among women. With these words of praise, Elizabeth tells Mary that she is special to God. Mary is the best example of discipleship for Christians of all ages, because she said yes to God. Elizabeth's words to Mary are part of the prayer called the Hail Mary.

December 25

The Nativity of the Lord
Christmas

Mass During the Night

First Reading (Isaiah 9:1-6)

The people who walked in darkness
    have seen a great light;
upon those who dwelt in the land of gloom
    a light has shone.
You have brought them abundant joy
    and great rejoicing,
as they rejoice before you as at the harvest,
    as people make merry when dividing spoils.
For the yoke that burdened them,
    the pole on their shoulder,
and the rod of their taskmaster
    you have smashed, as on the **day of Midian**.
For every boot that tramped in battle,
    every cloak rolled in blood,
    will be burned as fuel for flames.
For a child is born to us, a son is given us;
    upon his shoulder dominion rests.
They name him Wonder-Counselor, God-Hero,
    Father-Forever, Prince of Peace.
His dominion is vast
    and forever peaceful,
from David's throne, and over his kingdom,
    which he confirms and sustains
by judgment and justice,
    both now and forever.
The zeal of the Lord of hosts will do this!

The word of the Lord. **Thanks be to God.**

Responsorial Psalm (Psalm 96:1-2, 2-3, 11-12, 13)

R. **Today is born our Savior, Christ the Lord.**

Sing to the Lord a new song;
    sing to the Lord, all you lands.
Sing to the Lord; bless his name. R.

Announce his salvation, day after day.
   Tell his glory among the nations;
   among all peoples, his wondrous deeds. R.

Let the heavens be glad and the earth rejoice;
   let the sea and what fills it resound;
   let the plains be joyful and all that is in them!
Then shall all the trees of the forest **exult**. R.

They shall exult before the LORD, for he comes;
   for he comes to rule the earth.
He shall rule the world with justice
   and the peoples with his constancy. R.

Second Reading (Titus 2:11-14)

Beloved: The grace of God has appeared, saving all and training us to reject godless ways and worldly desires and to live temperately, justly, and devoutly in this age, as we await the blessed hope, the appearance of the glory of our great God and savior Jesus Christ, who gave himself for us to deliver us from all lawlessness and to cleanse for himself a people as his own, eager to do what is good.

The word of the Lord. **Thanks be to God.**

Gospel (Luke 2:1-14)

A reading from the holy Gospel according to Luke.
Glory to you, O Lord.

In those days a decree went out from Caesar Augustus that the whole world should be enrolled. This was the first enrollment, when Quirinius was governor of Syria. So all went to be enrolled, each to his own town. And Joseph too went up from Galilee from the town of Nazareth to Judea, to the city of David that is called Bethlehem, because he was of the house and family of David, to be enrolled with Mary, his betrothed, who was with child. While they were there, the time came for her to have her child, and she gave birth to her firstborn son. She wrapped him in swaddling clothes and laid him in a **manger**, because there was no room for them in the inn.

Now there were shepherds in that region living in the fields and keeping the night watch over their flock. The **angel of the Lord** appeared to them and the glory of the Lord shone around them, and they were struck with great fear. The angel said to them, "Do not be afraid; for behold, I proclaim to you good news of great joy that will be for all the people. For today in the city of David a savior has been born for you who is Christ and Lord. And this will be a sign for you: you will find an infant wrapped in swaddling clothes and lying in a manger." And suddenly there was a multitude of the heavenly host with the angel, praising God and saying:

"Glory to God in the highest
and on earth peace to those on whom his favor rests."

The Gospel of the Lord. **Praise to you, Lord Jesus Christ.**

Christmas Day is celebrated on December 25th, but the Christmas season lasts for up to three weeks, ending with the Baptism of Jesus in January. The liturgical color for this season is white, the color of joy and celebration.

Prophets like **Isaiah** were good men and women who spoke for God. Sometimes their messages were demanding: they asked people to change their lives and attitudes in order to grow closer to God. At other times, they brought words of comfort.

The Midianites were descendants of Abraham who became a people separate from Israel. They eventually conquered Israel and oppressed God's people for seven years. The **day of Midian** refers to the battle in which the Israelites, led by Gideon, freed themselves from the Midianites.

Glory to God in the highest and on earth peace to all people!

Merry Christmas!

We **sing for joy** because our hearts are full of happiness: God has come to be with his people. In today's Psalm, we see that all creation — even the trees! — rejoices and glories in the Lord.

A **manger** is a wooden crate filled with hay to feed the animals in a stable. The baby Jesus was placed in a manger soon after he was born. It is amazing that God would choose to be born in such a simple place.

An **Angel of the Lord** is a messenger of God. Angels appear many times in the Bible, as we see angels revealing God's plan in the lives of Jesus, Mary, and Joseph.

December 29

Holy Family of Jesus,
Mary & Joseph

These are the readings for Year C. The first reading, responsorial psalm, and second reading from Year A (Sirach 3:2-6, 12-14; Psalm 128:1-2, 3, 4-5; Colossians 3:12-21 or 3:12-17) may also be used.

First Reading (1 Samuel 1:20-22, 24-28)

In those days Hannah conceived, and at the end of her term bore a son whom she called Samuel, since she had asked the Lord for him. The next time her husband Elkanah was going up with the rest of his household to offer the customary sacrifice to the Lord and to fulfill his vows, Hannah did not go, explaining to her husband, "Once the child is weaned, I will take him to appear before the Lord and to remain there forever; I will offer him as a perpetual **nazirite**."

Once Samuel was weaned, Hannah brought him up with her, along with a three-year-old bull, an ephah* of flour, and a skin of wine, and presented him at the temple of the Lord in Shiloh. After the boy's father had sacrificed the young bull, Hannah, his mother, approached **Eli** and said: "Pardon, my lord! As you live, my lord, I am the woman who stood near you here, praying to the Lord. I prayed for this child, and the Lord granted my request. Now I, in turn, give him to the Lord; as long as he lives, he shall be dedicated to the Lord." Hannah left Samuel there.

The word of the Lord. **Thanks be to God.**

Responsorial Psalm (Psalm 84:2-3, 5-6, 9-10)

R. **Blessed are they who dwell in your house, O Lord.**

How lovely is your dwelling place, O Lord of hosts!
My soul yearns and pines for the courts of the Lord.
My heart and my flesh cry out for the living God. R.

Happy they who dwell in your house!
Continually they praise you.
Happy the men whose strength you are!
Their hearts are set upon the pilgrimage. R.

O Lord of hosts, hear our prayer;
hearken, O God of Jacob!
O God, behold our shield,
and look upon the face of your anointed. R.

Second Reading (1 John 3:1-2, 21-24)

Beloved: See what love the Father has bestowed on us that we may be called the children of God. And so we are. The reason **the world** does not know us is that it did not know him. Beloved, we are God's children now; what we shall be has not yet been revealed. We do know that when it is revealed we shall be like him, for we shall see him as he is.

Beloved, if our hearts do not condemn us, we have confidence in God and receive from him whatever we ask, because we keep his commandments and do what pleases him. And his commandment is this: we should believe in the name of his Son, Jesus Christ, and love one another just as he commanded us. Those who keep his commandments remain in him, and he in them, and the way we know that he remains in us is from the Spirit he gave us.

The word of the Lord. **Thanks be to God.**

Gospel (Luke 2:41-52)

A reading from the holy Gospel according to Luke.
Glory to you, O Lord.

Each year Jesus' parents went to Jerusalem for the feast of Passover, and when he was twelve years old, they went up according to festival custom. After they had completed its days, as they were returning, the boy Jesus remained behind in Jerusalem, but his parents did not know it. Thinking that he was in the caravan, they journeyed for a day and looked for him among their relatives and acquaintances, but not finding him, they returned to Jerusalem to look for him. After three days they found him in the temple, sitting in the midst of the **teachers**, listening to them and asking them questions, and all who heard him were astounded at his understanding and his answers. When his parents saw him, they were astonished, and his mother said to him, "Son, why have you done this to us? Your father and I have been looking for you with great anxiety." And he said to them, "Why were you looking for me? Did you not know that I must be in my Father's house?" But they did not understand what he said to them. He went down with them and came to Nazareth, and was obedient to them; and his mother kept all these things in her heart. And Jesus advanced in wisdom and age and favor before God and man.

The Gospel of the Lord. **Praise to you, Lord Jesus Christ.**

Key Words

Like the **Holy Family** of Jesus, Mary, and Joseph, our family is a gift from God. We take care of this gift and treasure it when we share our lives, listen to one another and pray together.

. . . .

Samuel, a prophet and judge in Israel, was born over 1,000 years before Jesus. The Lord chose Samuel to anoint Saul, the first king of Israel. Samuel also anointed David, who was king after Saul. The Bible contains two books in his name: 1 Samuel and 2 Samuel.

. . . .

A **nazirite** was a man who lived a special life of holiness. In Samuel's case, his mother, Hannah, had longed for a child but was childless. She promised God that if God gave her a son, she would offer him to God in this special way, as a nazirite. God heard and answered her prayer.

Eli was the chief priest at the sanctuary at Shiloh. His task was to guard the sanctuary, especially the Ark of the Covenant that was kept there.

. . . .

In this letter of Saint John, **the world** refers to people who think only about things like money and having fun. Worldly people often find it difficult to make room in their hearts for Jesus.

. . . .

The **teachers** in the temple were men who spent their lives studying the Bible and sharing their knowledge with the people. They were wise and highly respected, and not the usual companions for a child.

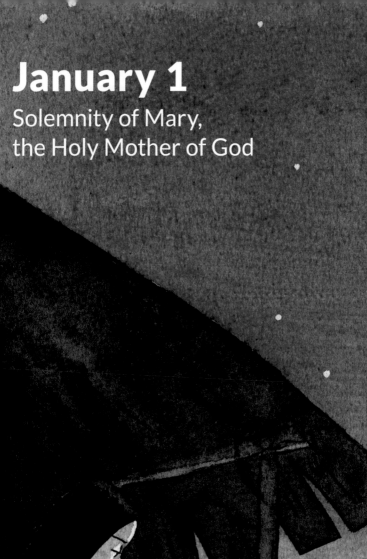

January 1

Solemnity of Mary,
the Holy Mother of God

First Reading (Numbers 6:22-27)

The Lord said to **Moses**: "Speak to **Aaron** and his sons and tell them: This is how you shall bless the Israelites. Say to them:

> The LORD bless you and keep you!
> The LORD let his face shine upon you,
>   and be gracious to you!
> The LORD look upon you kindly and give you peace!

So shall they invoke my name upon the **Israelites**, and I will bless them."

The word of the Lord. **Thanks be to God.**

Responsorial Psalm (Psalm 67:2-3, 5, 6, 8)

R. **May God bless us in his mercy.**

> May God have pity on us and bless us;
>   may he let his face shine upon us.
> So may your way be known upon earth;
>   among all nations, your salvation. R.

> May the nations be glad and exult
>   because you rule the peoples in **equity**;
>   the nations on the earth you guide. R.

> May the peoples praise you, O God;
>   may all the peoples praise you!
> May God bless us,
>   and may all the ends of the earth fear him! R.

Second Reading (Galatians 4:4-7)

Brothers and sisters: When the **fullness of time** had come, God sent his Son, born of a woman, born under the law, to ransom those under the law, so that we might receive adoption as sons. As proof that you are sons, God sent the Spirit of his Son into our hearts, crying out, "**Abba**, Father!" So you are no longer a slave but a son, and if a son then also an heir, through God.

The word of the Lord. **Thanks be to God.**

Gospel (Luke 2:16-21)

A reading from the holy Gospel according to Luke.
Glory to you, O Lord.

The shepherds went in haste to Bethlehem and found Mary and Joseph, and the infant lying in the **manger**. When they saw this, they made known the message that had been told them about this child. All who heard it were amazed by what had been told them by the shepherds. And Mary kept all these things, **reflecting** on them in her heart. Then the shepherds returned, glorifying and praising God for all they had heard and seen, just as it had been told to them.

When eight days were completed for his circumcision, he was named Jesus, the name given him by the angel before he was conceived in the womb.

The Gospel of the Lord. **Praise to you, Lord Jesus Christ.**

Key Words

The **book of Numbers** is found in the Hebrew Scriptures or Old Testament. It is called "Numbers" because it talks about many numbers and times when the people of Israel were counted. In Hebrew, it is called "In the Desert," because it tells of the travels of the Israelites after they left slavery in Egypt.

Moses was a friend of God who was born in Egypt when the Israelites were slaves there. When God asked him to lead the people to freedom, Moses said yes because he loved God and didn't want the people to suffer anymore. The people left Egypt on a journey called the "Exodus" about 1,250 years before the time of Jesus.

Aaron, Moses' older brother, helped him free the Israelites. When Moses went up Mount Sinai to receive God's law, Aaron stayed with the people.

To judge with **equity** is to be fair to everyone. In the Psalm, the Psalmist is praising God for God's fairness to all people on earth.

Fullness of time means when the time was right for God to send Jesus into the world.

In Aramaic, the language Jesus spoke, **Abba** means "Daddy." By calling God "Abba," Jesus shows that we can talk to God with the same trust and love that small children have for their father.

A **manger** is the place in a barn or stable for the animals' food. Its name is from the French word *manger,* to eat.

To **reflect** means to think about something a lot. Like all mothers, Mary remembered all the details surrounding the birth of her child.

January 5

The Epiphany of the Lord

First Reading (Isaiah 60:1-6)

Rise up in splendor, Jerusalem! Your light has come,
   the glory of the Lord shines upon you.
See, darkness covers the earth,
   and thick clouds cover the peoples;
but upon you the LORD shines,
   and over you appears his glory.
Nations shall walk by your light,
   and kings by your shining radiance.
Raise your eyes and look about;
   they all gather and come to you:
your sons come from afar,
   and your daughters in the arms of their nurses.

Then you shall be radiant at what you see,
   your heart shall throb and overflow,
for the riches of the sea shall be emptied out before you,
   the wealth of nations shall be brought to you.
Caravans of camels shall fill you,
   dromedaries from **Midian** and **Ephah**;
all from **Sheba** shall come
   bearing gold and frankincense,
   and proclaiming the praises of the LORD.

The word of the Lord. **Thanks be to God.**

Responsorial Psalm (Psalm 72:1-2, 7-8, 10-11, 12-13)

R. **Lord, every nation on earth will adore you.**

O God, with your judgment endow the king,
    and with your justice, the king's son;
he shall govern your people with justice
    and your afflicted ones with judgment. R.

Justice shall flower in his days,
    and profound peace, till the moon be no more.
May he rule from sea to sea,
    and from the River to the ends of the earth. R.

The kings of Tarshish* and the Isles shall offer gifts;
    the kings of Arabia and Seba shall bring tribute.
All kings shall pay him homage,
    all nations shall serve him. R.

For he shall rescue the poor when he cries out,
    and the afflicted when he has no one to help him.
He shall have pity for the lowly and the poor;
    the lives of the poor he shall save. R.

Second Reading (Ephesians 3:2-3a, 5-6)

Brothers and sisters: You have heard of the stewardship of
God's grace that was given to me for your benefit, namely,
that the **mystery** was made known to me by **revelation**. It was
not made known to people in other generations as it has now
been revealed to his holy apostles and prophets by the Spirit:
that the Gentiles are coheirs, members of the same body, and
copartners in the promise in Christ Jesus through the gospel.

The word of the Lord. **Thanks be to God.**

Gospel (Matthew 2:1-12)

A reading from the holy Gospel according to Matthew.
Glory to you, O Lord.

When Jesus was born in **Bethlehem of Judea**, in the days of King Herod, behold, magi from the east arrived in Jerusalem, saying, "Where is the newborn king of the Jews? We saw his star at its rising and have come to do him **homage**." When King Herod heard this, he was greatly troubled, and all Jerusalem with him. Assembling all the chief priests and the scribes of the people, he inquired of them where the Christ was to be born. They said to him, "In Bethlehem of Judea, for thus it has been written through the prophet:

And you, Bethlehem, land of Judah,
*   are by no means least among the rulers of Judah;*
since from you shall come a ruler,
*   who is to shepherd my people Israel."*

Then Herod called the magi secretly and ascertained from them the time of the star's appearance. He sent them to Bethlehem and said, "Go and search diligently for the child. When you have found him, bring me word, that I too may go and do him homage." After their audience with the king they set out. And behold, the star that they had seen at its rising preceded them, until it came and stopped over the place where the child was. They were overjoyed at seeing the star, and on entering the house they saw the child with Mary his mother. They prostrated themselves and did him homage. Then they opened their treasures and offered him gifts of **gold, frankincense, and myrrh**. And having been warned in a dream not to return to Herod, they departed for their country by another way.

The Gospel of the Lord. **Praise to you, Lord Jesus Christ.**

Key Words

Epiphany is a Greek word that means "unveiling," where something is revealed. God revealed his love for all people by sending us his Son, Jesus, as a baby.

Midian, Ephah and Sheba were three ancient kingdoms near Israel. In the book of the Prophet Isaiah in the Bible, they represent all the nations outside Israel.

The **Ephesians** were a group of Christians in the city of Ephesus. A letter Saint Paul wrote to them is now part of the Bible. Ephesus is located in modern-day Turkey.

A **mystery** is something that is very hard to understand. In Saint Paul's letter to the Ephesians, it means God's plan to create a human community in Christ.

To know something by **revelation** means that God has shown or given someone this knowledge.

Bethlehem of Judea is the city of King David, one of Jesus' ancestors. Joseph and Mary went to Bethlehem for a census (an official counting of all the people). Jesus was born during their stay there.

To pay someone **homage** is to show your respect or honor for them in a public way, such as by bowing or bringing gifts.

Gold, frankincense, and myrrh are three very expensive gifts: gold is a precious metal; frankincense and myrrh are rare, sweet-smelling incenses. Myrrh is the main ingredient in holy anointing oil.

January 12

The Baptism of the Lord

These are the readings for Year C. The first reading, responsorial psalm, and second reading from Year A (Isaiah 42:1-4, 6-7; Psalm 29:1-2, 3-4, 3, 9-10; and Acts 10:34-38) may also be used.

First Reading (Isaiah 40:1-5, 9-11)

Comfort, give comfort to my people,
　　says your God.
Speak tenderly to Jerusalem, and proclaim to her
　　　that her service is at an end,
　　　her guilt is expiated;
indeed, she has received from the hand of the LORD
　　　double for all her sins.

　　　　A voice cries out:
In the desert prepare the way of the LORD!
　　　Make straight in the wasteland a highway for our God!
Every valley shall be filled in,
　　　every mountain and hill shall be made low;
the rugged land shall be made a plain,
　　　the rough country, a broad valley.
Then the glory of the LORD shall be revealed,
　　　and all people shall see it together;
　　　for the mouth of the LORD has spoken.

Go up on to a high mountain,
　　　Zion,* herald of glad tidings;
cry out at the top of your voice,
　　　Jerusalem, herald of good news!
Fear not to cry out
　　　and say to the cities of **Judah**:
　　　Here is your God!
Here comes with power
　　　the Lord GOD,
　　　who rules by a strong arm;
here is his reward with him,
　　　his recompense before him.
Like a **shepherd** he feeds his flock;
　　　in his arms he gathers the lambs,
carrying them in his bosom,
　　　and leading the ewes with care.

The word of the Lord. **Thanks be to God.**

Responsorial Psalm
(Psalm 104:1b-2, 3-4, 24-25, 27-28, 29-30)

R. **O bless the Lord, my soul.**

O LORD, my God, you are great indeed!
    You are clothed with majesty and glory,
robed in light as with a cloak.
    You have spread out the heavens like a tent-cloth; R.

You have constructed your palace upon the waters.
    You make the clouds your chariot;
you travel on the wings of the wind.
    You make the winds your messengers,
and flaming fire your ministers. R.

How manifold are your works, O LORD!
    In wisdom you have wrought them all—
the earth is full of your creatures;
    the sea also, great and wide,
in which are schools without number
    of living things both small and great. R.

They look to you to give them food in due time.
    When you give it to them, they gather it;
when you open your hand, they are filled
    with good things. R.

If you take away their breath, they perish
        and return to the dust.
    When you send forth your spirit, they are created,
and you renew the face of the earth. R.

Second Reading (Titus 2:11-14; 3:4-7)

Beloved: The grace of God has appeared, saving all and training us to reject godless ways and **worldly desires** and to live **temperately**, justly, and devoutly in this age, as we await the blessed hope, the appearance of the glory of our great God and savior Jesus Christ, who gave himself for us to deliver us from all lawlessness and to cleanse for himself a people as his own, eager to do what is good.

> When the kindness and generous love
>   of God our savior appeared,
> not because of any righteous deeds we had done
>   but because of his **mercy**,
> he saved us through the bath of rebirth
>   and **renewal** by the Holy Spirit,
> whom he richly poured out on us
>   through Jesus Christ our savior,
> so that we might be justified by his grace
>   and become heirs in hope of eternal life.

The word of the Lord. **Thanks be to God.**

Gospel (Luke 3:15-16, 21-22)

A reading from the holy Gospel according to Luke.
Glory to you, O Lord.

The people were filled with expectation, and all were asking in their hearts whether **John** might be the Christ. John answered them all, saying, "I am baptizing you with water, but one mightier than I is coming. I am not worthy to loosen the thongs of his sandals. He will baptize you with the Holy Spirit and fire."

After all the people had been baptized and Jesus also had been baptized and was praying, heaven was opened and the Holy Spirit descended upon him in bodily form like a dove. And a voice came from heaven, "You are my beloved Son; **with you I am well pleased**."

The Gospel of the Lord. **Praise to you, Lord Jesus Christ.**

Key Words

Judah was one of the twelve sons of Jacob. Each son was the chief of one of the twelve tribes of Israel. The tribe of Judah established itself to the south of Jerusalem.

The Bible explains the great love of God (the **shepherd**) for us (his sheep). The shepherd cares for his sheep all day and night, finding pastures where there is grass to eat and water to drink.

Worldly desires arise when we live as if the most important thing in life is to please only ourselves. When we live in God's grace and accept his mercy, then we live as God's children and are a light to the world.

Saint Paul taught that we who are Jesus' friends should live without the need for so many things — we should live **temperately**. To be temperate is to eat and drink just what we need, and to enjoy ourselves without hurting ourselves or others.

Baptism brings us to **renewal.** It allows us to be "born" in a new way, united with the resurrected Jesus, among the great family of Christians which is the Church.

John the Baptist was the son of Zechariah and Elizabeth, who was a cousin of the Virgin Mary. He was known as "the precursor" because he preached that the Messiah was about to arrive. He was called John the Baptist because those who were converted by his preaching were baptized in order to prepare themselves for the coming of the Savior.

When today's gospel tells us that a voice from the sky said, "**with you I am well pleased,**" it is showing us that Jesus is the Son of God and has God's approval. Jesus came to teach us the way we should live as brothers and sisters — as children of God.

First Reading (Isaiah 62:1-5)

For **Zion's** sake I will not be silent,
for Jerusalem's sake I will not be quiet,
until her vindication shines forth like the dawn
    and her victory like a burning torch.

Nations shall behold your vindication,
    and all the kings your glory;
you shall be **called by a new name**
    pronounced by the mouth of the LORD.
You shall be a glorious crown in the hand of the LORD,
    a royal diadem held by your God.
No more shall people call you "Forsaken,"
    or your land "Desolate,"
but you shall be called "My Delight,"
    and your land "Espoused."
For the LORD delights in you
    and **makes your land his spouse**.
As a young man marries a virgin,
    your Builder shall **marry** you;
and as a bridegroom rejoices in his bride
    so shall your God rejoice in you.

The word of the Lord. **Thanks be to God.**

Responsorial Psalm (Psalm 96:1-2, 2-3, 7-8, 9-10)

R. **Proclaim his marvelous deeds to all the nations.**

Sing to the LORD a new song;
    sing to the LORD, all you lands.
Sing to the LORD; bless his name. R.

Announce his salvation, day after day.
Tell his glory among the nations;
    among all peoples, his wondrous deeds. R.

Give to the LORD, you families of nations,
    give to the LORD glory and praise;
    give to the LORD the glory due his name! R.

Worship the LORD in holy attire.
    Tremble before him, all the earth;
say among the nations: The LORD is king.
    He governs the peoples with equity. R.

Second Reading (1 Corinthians 12:4-11)

Brothers and sisters: There are different kinds of spiritual **gifts** but the same **Spirit**; there are different forms of service but the same Lord; there are different workings but the same God who produces all of them in everyone. To each individual the manifestation of the Spirit is given for some benefit. To one is given through the Spirit the expression of wisdom; to another, the expression of knowledge according to the same Spirit; to another, faith by the same Spirit; to another, gifts of healing by the one Spirit; to another, mighty deeds; to another, prophecy; to another, discernment of spirits; to another, varieties of tongues; to another, interpretation of tongues. But one and the same Spirit produces all of these, distributing them individually to each person as he wishes.

The word of the Lord. **Thanks be to God.**

Gospel (John 2:1-11)

A reading from the holy Gospel according to John.
Glory to you, O Lord.

There was a wedding at **Cana in Galilee**, and the mother of Jesus was there. Jesus and his disciples were also invited to the wedding. When the wine ran short, the mother of Jesus said to him, "They have no wine." And Jesus said to her, "Woman, how does your concern affect me? My hour has not yet come." His mother said to the servers, "Do whatever he tells you." Now there were six stone water jars there for Jewish ceremonial washings, each holding twenty to thirty gallons. Jesus told them, "Fill the jars with water." So they filled them to the brim. Then he told them, "Draw some out now and take it to the headwaiter." So they took it. And when the headwaiter tasted the water that had become wine, without knowing where it came from—although the servers who had drawn the water knew—, the headwaiter called the bridegroom and said to him, "Everyone serves good wine first, and then when people have drunk freely, an inferior one; but you have kept the good wine until now." Jesus did this as the beginning of his **signs** at Cana in Galilee and so revealed his glory, and his disciples began to believe in him.

The Gospel of the Lord. **Praise to you, Lord Jesus Christ.**

Key Words

Zion is the name of the ancient fort of Jerusalem, built on a hill of the same name. It is a way to refer to the entire city of Jerusalem.

When someone is **called by a new name,** we recognize that this person has changed for the better or is like a new person. The new name celebrates this change.

In the reading from Isaiah, the word **marry** is used to describe the deep love that God has for his people. Isaiah uses the love we feel for the person we marry as a way to help us understand God's love for us.

The **Corinthians** were members of a Christian community in Corinth that received several letters from Saint Paul. Corinth was the capital city of a Roman province in what is now Greece.

Saint Paul uses the word **gifts** to signify the qualities or skills that God gives to us. No two people are alike and all our gifts are different. Yet we all receive our gifts from the Spirit and are called to use our gifts for the good of the community.

The Holy **Spirit** is the power of God that is present in our lives. There are three persons in God: God the Father, Jesus the Son and the Holy Spirit. Jesus sent us his Spirit after he rose from the dead, to guide us and give us strength in following him.

Cana of Galilee is a town located near Nazareth. Jesus grew up in Nazareth, and when he went to Jerusalem people could tell he was from Galilee because of his accent and the way he spoke.

In John's Gospel, the miracles of Jesus are called **signs** — wonders he performed in order to encourage people to believe he was the one sent by God to save us.

January 26

3rd Sunday in Ordinary Time

First Reading (Nehemiah 8:2-4a, 5-6, 8-10)

Ezra the priest brought the law before the assembly, which consisted of men, women, and those children old enough to understand. Standing at one end of the open place that was before the Water Gate, he read out of the book from daybreak till midday, in the presence of the men, the women, and those children old enough to understand; and all the people listened attentively to the book of the law. Ezra the scribe stood on a wooden platform that had been made for the occasion. He opened the scroll so that all the people might see it—for he was standing higher up than any of the people—; and, as he opened it, all the people rose. Ezra blessed the LORD, the great God, and all the people, their hands raised high, answered, **"Amen, amen!"** Then they bowed down and prostrated themselves before the LORD, their faces to the ground. Ezra read plainly from the book of the law of God, interpreting it so that all could understand what was read. Then Nehemiah, that is, His Excellency, and Ezra the priest-scribe and the Levites* who were instructing the people said to all the people: "Today is holy to the LORD your God. Do not be sad, and do not weep"—for all the people were weeping as they heard the words of the law. He said further: "Go, eat rich foods and drink sweet drinks, and allot portions to those who had nothing prepared; for today is holy to our LORD. Do not be saddened this day, for rejoicing in the LORD must be your strength!"

The word of the Lord. **Thanks be to God.**

Responsorial Psalm (Psalm 19:8, 9, 10, 15)

R. **Your words, Lord, are Spirit and life.**

The law of the LORD is perfect,
    refreshing the soul;
the decree of the LORD is trustworthy,
    giving wisdom to the simple. R.

The precepts of the LORD are right,
    rejoicing the heart;
the command of the LORD is clear,
    enlightening the eye. R.

The fear of the LORD is pure,
> enduring forever;
the ordinances of the LORD are true,
> all of them just. R.

Let the words of my mouth and the thought of my heart
> find favor before you,
O LORD, my rock and my redeemer. R.

Second Reading (1 Corinthians 12:12-30)

For the shorter version, omit the indented parts in brackets.

Brothers and sisters: As a body is one though it has many parts, and all the parts of the body, though many, are one body, so also Christ. For in one Spirit we were all baptized into one body, whether Jews or Greeks, slaves or free persons, and we were all given to drink of one Spirit.

Now the body is not a single part, but many.

[If a foot should say, "Because I am not a hand I do not belong to the body," it does not for this reason belong any less to the body. Or if an ear should say, "Because I am not an eye I do not belong to the body," it does not for this reason belong any less to the body. If the whole body were an eye, where would the hearing be? If the whole body were hearing, where would the sense of smell be? But as it is, God placed the parts, each one of them, in the body as he intended. If they were all one part, where would the body be? But as it is, there are many parts, yet one body. The eye cannot say to the hand, "I do not need you," nor again the head to the feet, "I do not need you." Indeed, the parts of the body that seem to be weaker are all the more necessary, and those parts of the body that we consider less honorable we surround with greater honor, and our less presentable parts are treated with greater propriety, whereas our more presentable parts do not need this. But God has so constructed the body as to give greater honor to a part that is without it, so that there may be no division in the body, but that the parts may have the same concern for one another. If one part suffers, all the parts suffer with it; if one part is honored, all the parts share its joy.

Now] **you are Christ's body**, and individually parts of it.

[Some people God has designated in the church to be, first, apostles; second, prophets; third, teachers; then, mighty deeds; then gifts of healing, assistance, administration, and varieties of tongues. Are all apostles? Are all prophets? Are all teachers? Do all work mighty deeds? Do all have gifts of healing? Do all speak in tongues? Do all interpret?]

The word of the Lord. **Thanks be to God.**

Gospel (Luke 1:1-4; 4:14-21)

A reading from the holy Gospel according to Luke.
Glory to you, O Lord.

Since many have undertaken to compile a narrative of the events that have been fulfilled among us, just as those who were eyewitnesses from the beginning and ministers of the word have handed them down to us, I too have decided, after investigating everything accurately anew, to write it down in an orderly sequence for you, most excellent **Theophilus**, so that you may realize the certainty of the teachings you have received.

Jesus returned to Galilee in the power of the Spirit, and news of him spread throughout the whole region. He taught in their **synagogues** and was praised by all.

He came to Nazareth, where he had grown up, and went according to his custom into the synagogue on the sabbath day. He stood up to read and was handed a scroll of the prophet Isaiah. He unrolled the scroll and found the passage where it was written:

> The Spirit of the Lord is upon me,
>   because he has **anointed** me
>   to bring glad tidings to the poor.
> He has sent me to proclaim liberty to captives
>   and recovery of sight to the blind,
>   to let the oppressed go free,
>   and to proclaim a year acceptable to the Lord.

Rolling up the scroll, he handed it back to the attendant and sat down, and the eyes of all in the synagogue looked intently at him. He said to them, "Today this Scripture passage is fulfilled in your hearing."

The Gospel of the Lord. **Praise to you, Lord Jesus Christ.**

Key Words

Ezra was a holy priest who, together with Nehemiah, encouraged the people to rebuild the city of Jerusalem 515 years before the birth of Christ. He also urged the people to respect the Scriptures and to recommit themselves to their covenant with God.

Amen is the Hebrew word meaning "yes," "I agree," "I promise." When we say it twice, we are emphasizing our agreement — we really mean what we say.

Saint Paul compares the Church to a body. Christ is the head, and we the people **are the body of Christ.** By this comparison we understand that Christ is most important; but just as the head needs the body, so we are all important to the life of the Church.

The **Gospel according to Luke** was written for Christians who were not Jewish. It is also known as the Gospel of mercy. Saint Luke wrote the Acts of the Apostles as well.

Theophilus literally means "friend or beloved of God" in Greek. This person was a representative of the Christian communities of Greece. Saint Luke addressed his gospel as well as the Acts of the Apostles to Theophilus.

Synagogues are buildings that serve as meeting places for the Jewish community to pray and read the Scriptures together. They are like the churches or temples in other faiths.

February 2
Presentation of the Lord

First Reading (Malachi 3:1-4)

Thus says the Lord GOD:
Lo, I am sending my messenger
    to prepare the way before me;
And suddenly there will come to the temple
    the LORD whom you seek,
And the messenger of the **covenant** whom you desire.
    Yes, he is coming, says the LORD of hosts.
But who will endure the day of his coming?
    And who can stand when he appears?
For he is like the **refiner's fire**,
    or like the fuller's lye.
He will sit refining and purifying silver,
    and he will purify the sons of Levi,
Refining them like gold or like silver
    that they may offer due sacrifice to the LORD.
Then the sacrifice of Judah and Jerusalem
    will please the LORD,
    as in the days of old, as in years gone by.

The word of the Lord. **Thanks be to God.**

Responsorial Psalm (Psalm 24:7, 8, 9, 10)

R. **Who is this king of glory? It is the Lord!**

Lift up, O gates, your lintels;
    reach up, you ancient portals,
    that the king of glory may come in! R.

Who is this king of glory?
    The LORD, strong and mighty,
    the LORD, mighty in battle. R.

Lift up, O gates, your lintels;
    reach up, you ancient portals,
    that the king of glory may come in! R.

Who is this king of glory?
    The LORD of hosts; he is the king of glory. R.

Second Reading (Hebrews 2:14-18)

Since the children share in blood and flesh,
Jesus likewise shared in them,
that through death he might destroy the one
who has the power of death, that is, the Devil,
and free those who through fear of death
had been subject to slavery all their life.
Surely he did not help angels
but rather the descendants of **Abraham**;
therefore, he had to become like his brothers and sisters
in every way,
that he might be a merciful and faithful high priest before God
to expiate the sins of the people.
Because he himself was tested through what he suffered,
he is able to help those who are being tested.

The word of the Lord. **Thanks be to God.**

Gospel (Luke 2:22-40 or Luke 2:22-32)

When the days were completed for their purification
according to the law of Moses,
Mary and Joseph took Jesus up to Jerusalem
to present him to the Lord,
just as it is written in the law of the Lord,
Every male that opens the womb shall be consecrated to the Lord,
and to offer the sacrifice of
a pair of **turtledoves** *or two young pigeons,*
in accordance with the dictate in the law of the Lord.

Now there was a man in Jerusalem whose name was Simeon.
This man was righteous and devout,
awaiting the consolation of Israel,
and the Holy Spirit was upon him.
It had been revealed to him by the Holy Spirit
that he should not see death
before he had seen the Christ of the Lord.
He came in the Spirit into the temple;
and when the parents brought in the child Jesus
to perform the custom of the law in regard to him,
he took him into his arms and blessed God, saying:

"Now, Master, you may let your servant go
  in peace, according to your word,
for my eyes have seen your salvation,
  which you prepared in sight of all the peoples,
a light for revelation to the Gentiles,
  and glory for your people Israel."

The child's father and mother were amazed at what was said
    about him;
and Simeon blessed them and said to Mary his mother,
"Behold, this child is destined
for the fall and rise of many in Israel,
and to be a sign that will be contradicted
—and you yourself a sword will pierce—
so that the thoughts of many hearts may be revealed."
There was also a prophetess, Anna,
  the daughter of Phanuel, of the **tribe of Asher**.
She was advanced in years,
  having lived seven years with her husband after her marriage,
  and then as a widow until she was eighty-four.
She never left the temple,
  but worshiped night and day with fasting and prayer.
And coming forward at that very time,
  she gave thanks to God and spoke about the child
  to all who were awaiting the redemption of Jerusalem.

When they had fulfilled all the prescriptions
  of the law of the Lord,
  they returned to Galilee, to their own town of Nazareth.
The child grew and became strong, filled with wisdom;
  and the favor of God was upon him.

The Gospel of the Lord. **Praise to you, Lord Jesus Christ.**

A **covenant** is a special kind of promise or agreement. In the Bible, God often makes a covenant with an individual or, sometimes, with whole groups of people. In the story of Noah's Ark, for example, God creates a rainbow as a sign of his promise to the world that he will never again flood all the earth.

A **refiner's fire** is used to clean precious metals such as silver and gold. Heating helps to separate out any other materials, making sure that the metal becomes as pure, and valuable, as possible.

Abraham is one of the most important people in the Bible. He was a man of great faith. We read his story in the Book of Genesis, which tells how God makes a special call to Abraham, promising him land and offspring if he obeys. Because Abraham listens to God, God blesses him with a son, Isaac. He is seen as the father of the people of Israel, and our father in faith.

A relative of the pigeon, a **turtledove** has a lovely song and a gentle nature. Because they often are found in pairs, many people see turtledoves as a sign of love and devotion. In biblical times, a turtledove was seen as a pure animal, which is why it was used in sacrifices.

Abraham's grandson was named Jacob. Jacob was also known as Israel. Jacob had 12 sons, each of whom became the head of a tribe, or family, of Israel. The **tribe of Asher** was made up of the family of Asher, Jacob's second son. The name Asher means blessing.

February 9

5th Sunday in Ordinary Time

First Reading (Isaiah 6:1-2a, 3-8)

In the year **King Uzziah** died, I saw the Lord seated on a high and lofty throne, with the train of his garment filling the temple. Seraphim were stationed above.

They cried one to the other, "Holy, holy, holy is the Lord of hosts! All the earth is filled with his **glory**!" At the sound of that cry, the frame of the door shook and the house was filled with smoke.

Then I said, "Woe is me, I am doomed! For I am a man of unclean lips, living among a people of unclean lips; yet my eyes have seen the King, the Lord of hosts!" Then one of the seraphim flew to me, holding an **ember** that he had taken with tongs from the altar.

He touched my mouth with it, and said, "See, now that this has touched your lips, your wickedness is removed, your sin purged."

Then I heard the voice of the Lord saying, "Whom shall I send? Who will go for us?" "**Here I am**," I said; "**send me**!"

The word of the Lord. **Thanks be to God.**

Responsorial Psalm (Psalm 138:1-2, 2-3, 4-5, 7-8)

R. **In the sight of the angels I will sing your praises, Lord.**

I will give thanks to you, O Lord, with all my heart,
  for you have heard the words of my mouth;
  in the presence of the angels I will sing your praise;
I will worship at your holy temple
  and give thanks to your name. R.

Because of your kindness and your truth;
  for you have made great above all things
  your name and your promise.
When I called, you answered me;
  you built up strength within me. R.

All the kings of the earth shall give thanks to you, O Lord,
  when they hear the words of your mouth;
and they shall sing of the ways of the Lord:
  "Great is the glory of the Lord." R.

> Your right hand saves me.
>   The LORD will complete what he has done for me;
> your kindness, O LORD, endures forever;
>   forsake not the work of your hands. R.

Second Reading (1 Corinthians 15:1-11)

For the shorter version, omit the indented parts in brackets.

[I am reminding you, brothers and sisters, of the gospel I preached to you, which you indeed received and in which you also stand. Through it you are also being saved, if you hold fast to the word I preached to you, unless you believed in vain. For]

(Brothers and sisters,) I handed on to you as of first importance what I also received: that Christ died for our sins in accordance with the Scriptures; that he was buried; that he was raised on the third day in accordance with the Scriptures; that he appeared to Cephas, then to the Twelve. After that, he appeared to more than five hundred brothers at once, most of whom are still living, though some have fallen asleep. After that he appeared to James, then to all the apostles. Last of all, as to one **born abnormally**, he appeared to me.

[For I am the least of the apostles, not fit to be called an apostle, because I persecuted the church of God. But by the grace of God I am what I am, and his grace to me has not been ineffective. Indeed, I have toiled harder than all of them; not I, however, but the grace of God that is with me.]

Therefore, whether it be I or they, so we preach and so you believed.

The word of the Lord. **Thanks be to God.**

Gospel (Luke 5:1-11)

A reading from the holy Gospel according to Luke.
Glory to you, O Lord.

While the crowd was pressing in on Jesus and listening to the word of God, he was standing by the **Lake of Gennesaret**. He saw two boats there alongside the lake; the fishermen had disembarked and were washing their nets. Getting into one of the boats, the one belonging to Simon, he asked him to put out a short distance from the shore. Then he sat down and taught the crowds from the boat. After he had finished speaking, he said to Simon, "Put out into deep water and lower your nets for a catch." Simon said in reply, "Master, we have worked hard all night and have caught nothing, but at your command I will lower the nets." When they had done this, they caught a great number of fish and their nets were tearing. They signaled to their partners in the other boat to come to help them. They came and filled both boats so that the boats were in danger of sinking. When Simon Peter saw this, he fell at the knees of Jesus and said, "Depart from me, Lord, for I am a sinful man." For astonishment at the catch of fish they had made seized him and all those with him, and likewise James and John, the sons of Zebedee, who were partners of Simon. Jesus said to Simon, "Do not be afraid; from now on you will be **catching men**." When they brought their boats to the shore, they left everything and followed him.

The Gospel of the Lord. **Praise to you, Lord Jesus Christ.**

Key Words

King Uzziah was a king of Judah who reigned for over 50 years, 800 years before the birth of Christ. He brought peace and prosperity to his people, but he became very proud at the end of his life and was banished from the Temple.

. . . .

When we use the word **"glory"** to refer to God, we are saying that we recognize God's power and importance, greatness and splendor.

. . . .

An **ember** is a piece of red-hot charcoal. When the angel "burned" Isaiah's lips with a live coal, it represented his cleansing from sin. Isaiah was so happy because he then knew that God had forgiven him his sins.

. . . .

When Isaiah saw how his sins were forgiven and how great God's love was, he responded by saying, **"Here am I; send me!"** When we receive absolution in the Sacrament of Reconciliation, this should be our response, too.

Born abnormally was Saint Paul's way of recognizing that, by the grace of God, there had been a huge change in his life and he was reborn. He humbly accepted that this change was not due to his own efforts: his conversion was a special gift of grace from God.

. . . .

The **Lake of Gennesaret** was also known as the Sea of Galilee or the Sea of Tiberias. It was the scene of many of Jesus' actions (such as preaching from a boat to the people on shore, the miracle of calming the stormy seas, and the miracle of the loaves and fish). Jesus was also seen there after his resurrection.

. . . .

When Jesus told Simon Peter, a fisherman, that he would now be **catching people,** Jesus did not explain what this meant. But Simon Peter came to know that he was invited to dedicate his life so that others might know the Good News about the kingdom of God.

February 16

6th Sunday in Ordinary Time

First Reading (Jeremiah 17:5-8)

Thus says the LORD:

Cursed is the one who trusts in human beings,
  who seeks his strength in flesh,
  whose heart turns away from the LORD.
He is like a **barren bush in the desert**
  that enjoys no change of season,
but stands in a lava waste,
  a salt and empty earth.
Blessed is the one who trusts in the LORD,
  whose hope is the LORD.
He is like a tree planted beside the waters
  that stretches out its roots to the stream:
it fears not the heat when it comes;
  its leaves stay green;
in the year of drought it shows no distress,
  but still bears fruit.

The word of the Lord. **Thanks be to God.**

Responsorial Psalm (Psalm 1:1-2, 3, 4, 6)

R. **Blessed are they who hope in the Lord.**

Blessed the man who follows not
  the counsel of the wicked,
nor walks in the way of sinners,
  nor sits in the company of the insolent,
but delights in the law of the LORD
  and meditates on his law day and night. R.

He is like a tree
  planted near running water,
that yields its fruit in due season,
  and whose leaves never fade.
Whatever he does, prospers. R.

Not so the wicked, not so;
  they are like chaff which the wind drives away.
For the LORD watches over the way of the just,
  but the way of the wicked vanishes. R.

livingwithchrist.us

Second Reading (1 Corinthians 15:12, 16-20)

Brothers and sisters: If Christ is preached as **raised from the dead**, how can some among you say there is no resurrection of the dead? If the dead are not raised, neither has Christ been raised, and if Christ has not been raised, your faith is **vain**; you are still in your sins. Then those who have fallen asleep in Christ have perished. If for this life only we have hoped in Christ, we are the most pitiable people of all.

But now Christ has been raised from the dead, the **firstfruits** of those who have fallen asleep.

The word of the Lord. **Thanks be to God.**

Gospel (Luke 6:17, 20-26)

A reading from the holy Gospel according to Luke.
Glory to you, O Lord.

Jesus came down with the Twelve and stood on a stretch of level ground with a great crowd of his disciples and a large number of the people from all Judea and Jerusalem and the coastal region of Tyre and Sidon. And raising his eyes toward his disciples he said:

"Blessed are you who are poor,
　　for the kingdom of God is yours.
Blessed are you who are now hungry,
　　for you will be satisfied.
Blessed are you who are now weeping,
　　for you will laugh.

Blessed are you when people hate you, and when they exclude and insult you, and denounce your name as evil on account of the Son of Man. Rejoice and leap for joy on that day! Behold, your reward will be great in heaven. For their ancestors treated the prophets in the same way. But woe to you who are rich, for you have received your consolation.

Woe to you who are filled now,
　　for you will be hungry.
Woe to you who laugh now,
　　for you will grieve and weep.
Woe to you when all speak well of you,
　　for their ancestors treated the false prophets in this way."

The Gospel of the Lord. **Praise to you, Lord Jesus Christ.**

Jeremiah was born 645 years before Christ. While still a boy, Jeremiah was called by God to be a guide for the people of Israel. He preached against idolatry (the worship of false gods). There was a time when he suffered the rejection of many, including his own family. Yet, when it seemed that the people of Israel were reaching their end, Jeremiah encouraged them with the hope that God would never abandon them.

When Jeremiah compares the heart of a person who is far from God to a **barren bush in the desert,** or a thorny plant in dry land, he makes us realize the sadness we feel when we behave badly and how life is drained from our hearts when we turn from God.

Salt land is useless for agriculture, because the salt will not allow plants to grow. This is another way to describe the emptiness felt by those people who remain far from God.

When we say that Christ is **raised from the dead,** we are affirming the most wonderful thing in the world! Yes, Jesus died on the cross. But death, which appeared to be inevitable and to always triumph in the end, was overcome. We rejoice because all of us who are close to Jesus will also rise again at the end of time.

Saint Paul says our Christian faith would be **vain** or useless if Jesus had not risen from the dead. It is Jesus' triumph over death and the hope of the resurrection that give meaning and hope to our faith.

Firstfruits are the first of a crop to be harvested. In many religions, the first fruits have a religious significance and are offered as a sacrifice of thanks to the gods. Because Jesus is the first to rise from the dead, Saint Paul calls him the first fruits of those who have died.

February 23
7th Sunday in Ordinary Time

First Reading (1 Samuel 26:2, 7-9, 12-13, 22-23)

In those days, **Saul** went down to the desert of Ziph with three thousand picked men of Israel, to search for **David** in the desert of Ziph. So David and Abishai went among Saul's soldiers by night and found Saul lying asleep within the barricade, with his spear thrust into the ground at his head and Abner and his men sleeping around him.

Abishai whispered to David: "God has delivered your enemy into your grasp this day. Let me nail him to the ground with one thrust of the spear; I will not need a second thrust!" But David said to Abishai, "Do not harm him, for who can lay hands on the Lord's **anointed** and remain unpunished?" So David took the spear and the water jug from their place at Saul's head, and they got away without anyone's seeing or knowing or awakening. All remained asleep, because the Lord had put them into a deep slumber.

Going across to an opposite slope, David stood on a remote hilltop at a great distance from Abner, son of Ner, and the troops. He said: "Here is the king's spear. Let an attendant come over to get it. The Lord will reward each man for his justice and faithfulness. Today, though the Lord delivered you into my grasp, I would not harm the Lord's anointed."

The word of the Lord. **Thanks be to God.**

Responsorial Psalm (Psalm 103:1-2, 3-4, 8, 10, 12-13)

R. **The Lord is kind and merciful.**

Bless the Lord, O my soul;
and all my being, bless his holy name.
Bless the Lord, O my soul,
and forget not all his benefits. R.

He pardons all your iniquities,
heals all your ills.
He redeems your life from destruction,
crowns you with kindness and compassion. R.

Merciful and gracious is the LORD,
>   slow to anger and abounding in kindness.
Not according to our sins does he deal with us,
>   nor does he requite us according to our crimes. R.

As far as the east is from the west,
>   so far has he put our transgressions from us.
As a father has compassion on his children,
>   so the LORD has compassion on those who fear him. R.

Second Reading (1 Corinthians 15:45-49)

Brothers and sisters: It is written, *The first man, Adam, became a living being,* the **last Adam** a life-giving spirit. But the spiritual was not first; rather the natural and then the spiritual. The first man was from the earth, earthly; the second man, from heaven. As was the earthly one, so also are the earthly, and as is the heavenly one, so also are the heavenly. Just as we have borne the image of the earthly one, we shall also bear the image of the heavenly one.

The word of the Lord. **Thanks be to God.**

Gospel (Luke 6:27-38)

A reading from the holy Gospel according to Luke.
Glory to you, O Lord.

Jesus said to his disciples: "To you who hear I say, **love your enemies**, do good to those who hate you, bless those who curse you, pray for those who mistreat you. To the person who strikes you on one cheek, offer the other one as well, and from the person who takes your cloak, do not withhold even your tunic. Give to everyone who asks of you, and from the one who takes what is yours do not demand it back. Do to others as you would have them do to you. For if you love those who love you, what credit is that to you? Even sinners love those who love them. And if you do good to those who do good to you, what credit is that to you? Even sinners do the same. If you lend money to those from whom you expect repayment, what credit is that to you? Even sinners lend to sinners, and get back the same amount. But rather, love your enemies and do good to them, and lend expecting nothing back; then your reward will be great and you will be children of **the Most High**, for he himself is kind to the ungrateful and the wicked. Be merciful, just as your Father is merciful.

"Stop judging and you will not be judged. Stop condemning and you will not be condemned. Forgive and you will be forgiven. Give, and gifts will be given to you; a good measure, packed together, shaken down, and overflowing, will be poured into your lap. For the measure with which you measure will in return be measured out to you."

The Gospel of the Lord. **Praise to you, Lord Jesus Christ.**

Key Words

Saul was the first king of Israel, from the year 1030 until 1010 before Christ. Although he was a good soldier, the Bible tells us that Saul had such a stubborn character that God would have preferred him not to be king. He died alongside three of his sons in a battle against the Philistines.

David was the second king of Israel, from the year 1010 to 970 before Christ. David had musical talent and was the hero who killed the giant Goliath. Although he committed serious errors a few times during his reign, he was well-loved by the people.

In the Bible, to **anoint** or smear someone's head with oil was to signify that they were being given a mission from God. Kings, prophets, and priests were anointed. The word Christ means "anointed one." We call Jesus the Christ because he was King, Prophet, and Priest.

Jesus was called the **last Adam** because he was the one who atoned for the first Adam's sin and made it possible for us to live fully the life God wants for us.

The commandment to **love your enemies** is very important in the teachings of Jesus. He himself lived by this hard teaching, even when he was suffering on the cross before his death.

Most High is a name given to God, to indicate that God is above all the angels and saints in heaven. In the early days of God's people, it also meant that God was above all other gods who were worshipped by Israel's neighbors and enemies.

livingwithchrist.us

103

March 2

8th Sunday in Ordinary Time

First Reading (Sirach 27:4-7)

When a **sieve** is shaken, the **husks** appear;
    so do one's faults when one speaks.
As the test of what the potter molds is in the **furnace**,
    so in tribulation is the test of the just.
The fruit of a tree shows the care it has had;
    so too does one's speech disclose the bent of one's mind.
Praise no one before he speaks,
    for it is then that people are tested.

The word of the Lord. **Thanks be to God.**

Responsorial Psalm (Psalm 92:2-3, 13-14, 15-16)

R. **Lord, it is good to give thanks to you.**

It is good to give thanks to the LORD,
    to sing praise to your name, Most High,
to proclaim your kindness at dawn
    and your faithfulness throughout the night. R.

The just one shall flourish like the palm tree,
    like a cedar of Lebanon shall he grow.
They that are planted in the house of the LORD
    shall flourish in the courts of our God. R.

They shall bear fruit even in old age;
    vigorous and sturdy shall they be,
declaring how just is the LORD,
    my rock, in whom there is no wrong. R.

Second Reading (1 Corinthians 15:54-58)

Brothers and sisters: When this which is corruptible clothes itself with incorruptibility and this which is mortal clothes itself with immortality, then the word that is written shall come about:

Death is swallowed up in victory.
Where, O death, is your victory?
Where, O death, is your sting?

The sting of death is sin, and the power of sin is the law. But thanks be to God who gives us the victory through our Lord Jesus Christ.

Therefore, my beloved brothers and sisters, be firm, steadfast, always fully devoted to the work of the Lord, knowing that in the Lord your labor is not in vain.

The word of the Lord. **Thanks be to God.**

Gospel (Luke 6:39-45)

A reading from the holy Gospel according to Luke.
Glory to you, O Lord.

Jesus told his disciples a parable, "Can a blind person guide a blind person? Will not both fall into a pit? No disciple is superior to the teacher; but when fully trained, every disciple will be like his teacher. Why do you notice the splinter in your brother's eye, but do not perceive the wooden beam in your own? How can you say to your brother, 'Brother, let me remove that splinter in your eye,' when you do not even notice the wooden beam in your own eye? You **hypocrite**! Remove the wooden beam from your eye first; then you will see clearly to remove the splinter in your brother's eye.

"A good tree does not bear rotten fruit, nor does a rotten tree bear good fruit. For every tree is known by its own fruit. For people do not pick figs from thornbushes, nor do they gather grapes from **brambles**. A good person out of the store of goodness in his heart produces good, but an evil person out of a store of evil produces evil; for from the fullness of the heart the mouth speaks."

The Gospel of the Lord. **Praise to you, Lord Jesus Christ.**

Key Words

A **sieve** is a fine strainer used to separate or filter materials. A baker sifts flour in a sieve, to remove the lumps. A prospector uses a sieve to find gold in mud. In the process, the good or useful is separated from the part that can be discarded.

Husks are an inedible part of a grain and are usually placed in the garbage or trash. The husks are not wanted. Sirach compares our faults to refuse — truly things that we should put aside.

A **furnace** is an oven used by potters to fire or bake clay. If the pot is well formed and the clay is of good quality, then the furnace will not damage the pot but rather strengthen it. If the clay or the workmanship is poor, the heat will show the weaknesses and the pot will be ruined. In this way, the pot is tested by fire.

A **hypocrite** is someone who says one thing but does another. They may say they love God, but they don't act in a loving way. Such behavior demeans the person, hurts others, and insults God.

A **bramble** is a tangled bush with many thorns. Some farmers consider it to be a weed and will remove it so that fruit-bearing plants can thrive. No farmer would expect to get figs or grapes from a bramble bush!

March 5

Ash Wednesday

First Reading (Joel 2:12-18)

Even now, says the LORD,
return to me with your whole heart,
    with fasting, and weeping, and mourning;
Rend your hearts, not your garments,
    and return to the LORD, your God.
For gracious and merciful is he,
    slow to anger, rich in kindness,
    and relenting in punishment.
Perhaps he will again relent
    and leave behind him a blessing,
Offerings and libations
    for the LORD, your God.

Blow the trumpet in Zion!*
    proclaim a fast,
    call an assembly;
Gather the people,
    notify the **congregation**;
Assemble the elders,
    gather the children
    and the infants at the breast;
Let the bridegroom quit his room
    and the bride her chamber.
Between the porch and the altar
    let the priests, the ministers of the LORD, weep,
And say, "Spare, O LORD, your people,
    and make not your heritage a reproach,
    with the nations ruling over them!
Why should they say among the peoples,
    'Where is their God?' "

Then the LORD was stirred to concern for his land
    and took pity on his people.

The word of the Lord. **Thanks be to God.**

Responsorial Psalm (Psalm 51:3-4, 5-6ab, 12-13, 14, 17)

R. **Be merciful, O Lord, for we have sinned.**

Have mercy on me, O God, in your goodness;
    in the greatness of your compassion
        wipe out my offense.
Thoroughly wash me from my guilt
    and of my sin cleanse me. R.

For I acknowledge my offense,
    and my sin is before me always:
"Against you only have I sinned,
    and done what is evil in your sight." R.

A clean heart create for me, O God,
    and a steadfast spirit renew within me.
Cast me not out from your presence,
    and your Holy Spirit take not from me. R.

Give me back the joy of your salvation,
    and a willing spirit sustain in me.
O Lord, open my lips,
    and my mouth shall proclaim your praise. R.

Second Reading (2 Corinthians 5:20–6:2)

Brothers and sisters: We are **ambassadors** for Christ, as if God were appealing through us. We implore you on behalf of Christ, be **reconciled** to God. For our sake he made him to be sin who did not know sin, so that we might become the righteousness of God in him.

Working together, then, we appeal to you not to receive the grace of God in vain. For he says:

In an acceptable time I heard you,
    and on the day of salvation I helped you.

Behold, now is a very acceptable time; behold, now is the day of salvation.

The word of the Lord. **Thanks be to God.**

Gospel (Matthew 6:1-6, 16-18)

A reading from the holy Gospel according to Matthew.
Glory to you, O Lord.

Jesus said to his disciples: "Take care not to perform righteous deeds in order that people may see them; otherwise, you will have no recompense from your heavenly Father. When you give alms, do not blow a trumpet before you, as the hypocrites do in the synagogues and in the streets to win the praise of others. Amen, I say to you, they have received their reward. But when you **give alms**, do not let your left hand know what your right is doing, so that your almsgiving may be secret. And your Father who sees in secret will repay you.

"When you **pray**, do not be like the hypocrites, who love to stand and pray in the synagogues and on street corners so that others may see them. Amen, I say to you, they have received their reward. But when you pray, go to your inner room, close the door, and pray to your Father in secret. And your Father who sees in secret will repay you.

"When you **fast**, do not look gloomy like the hypocrites. They neglect their appearance, so that they may appear to others to be fasting. Amen, I say to you, they have received their reward. But when you fast, anoint your head and wash your face, so that you may not appear to be fasting, except to your Father who is hidden. And your Father who sees what is hidden will repay you."

The Gospel of the Lord. **Praise to you, Lord Jesus Christ.**

Key Words

Ash Wednesday marks the beginning of Lent. Ashes are used as a sign of our sorrow for having turned away from God; they are placed on our forehead in the sign of the cross and we keep them until they wear off. The ashes are often produced by burning palms from the previous year's Passion (Palm) Sunday celebration.

. . . .

To **rend** something is to tear it apart forcefully. In biblical times, people would tear their clothing and cover themselves with ashes as signs of their repentance or sorrow. The Prophet Joel is saying that God would rather we rend or open our hearts as a sign of our willingness to return to God.

. . . .

A **congregation** is a gathering of people, usually for worship. In the Hebrew Scriptures, it can also mean the whole people of God.

. . . .

Ambassadors are messengers who have special authority to deliver a message or speak on

someone else's behalf. Saint Paul is telling us that we have a role to play as followers of Christ: we are chosen to spread the Good News. If we are to be faithful messengers, then we must open our hearts and be reconciled to God.

. . . .

To be **reconciled** means to be "at-one" with someone, by making up for something wrong we may have done. Through his death, Jesus makes up for our sins and we are reconciled with God.

. . . .

To **give alms** is to give money to the poor. The word comes from the Greek word for compassion or pity.

. . . .

The three traditional Lenten practices are **prayer, fasting** and **almsgiving**. We look inward through prayer and fasting, and look outward through almsgiving. During Lent, we not only focus on our own spiritual life; we also make a special effort to help those around us who are in need.

livingwithchrist.us

March 9
1st Sunday of Lent

First Reading (Deuteronomy 26:4-10)

Moses spoke to the people, saying: "The priest shall receive the basket from you and shall set it in front of the **altar** of the LORD, your God. Then you shall declare before the LORD, your God, 'My father was a wandering **Aramean** who went down to Egypt with a small household and lived there as an alien. But there he became a nation great, strong, and numerous. When the Egyptians maltreated and oppressed us, imposing hard labor upon us, we cried to the LORD, the God of our fathers, and he heard our cry and saw our affliction, our toil, and our oppression. He brought us out of Egypt with his strong hand and outstretched arm, with terrifying power, with signs and wonders; and bringing us into this country, he gave us this land flowing with milk and honey. Therefore, I have now brought you the firstfruits of the products of the soil which you, O LORD, have given me.' And having set them before the LORD, your God, you shall **bow down** in his presence."

The word of the Lord. **Thanks be to God.**

Responsorial Psalm (Psalm 91:1-2, 10-11, 12-13, 14-15)

R. **Be with me, Lord, when I am in trouble.**

You who dwell in the shelter of the Most High,
  who abide in the shadow of the Almighty,
say to the LORD, "My refuge and fortress,
  my God in whom I trust." R.

No evil shall befall you,
  nor shall affliction come near your tent,
for to his angels he has given command about you,
  that they guard you in all your ways. R.

Upon their hands they shall bear you up,
  lest you dash your foot against a stone.
You shall tread upon the asp and the viper;
  you shall trample down the lion and the dragon. R.

Because he clings to me, I will deliver him;
    I will set him on high because he acknowledges
        my name.
He shall call upon me, and I will answer him;
    I will be with him in distress;
I will deliver him and glorify him. R̸.

Second Reading (Romans 10:8-13)

Brothers and sisters: What does Scripture say?

The word is near you,
    in your mouth and in your heart—

that is, the word of faith that we preach—, for, if you **confess** with your mouth that Jesus is Lord and believe in your heart that God raised him from the dead, you will be saved. For one believes with the heart and so is justified, and one confesses with the mouth and so is saved. For the Scripture says, *No one who believes in him will be put to shame.* For there is no distinction between Jew and Greek; the same Lord is Lord of all, enriching all who call upon him. For "everyone who calls on the name of the Lord will be saved."

The word of the Lord. **Thanks be to God.**

Gospel (Luke 4:1-13)

A reading from the holy Gospel according to Luke.
Glory to you, O Lord.

Filled with the Holy Spirit, Jesus returned from the Jordan and was led by the Spirit into the desert for forty days, to be tempted by the **devil**. He ate nothing during those days, and when they were over he was hungry. The devil said to him, "If you are the Son of God, command this stone to become bread." Jesus answered him, "It is written, *One does not live on bread alone.*" Then he took him up and showed him all the kingdoms of the world in a single instant. The devil said to him, "I shall give to you all this power and glory; for it has been handed over to me, and I may give it to whomever I wish. All this will be yours, if you worship me." Jesus said to him in reply, "It is written:

> *You shall worship the Lord, your God,*
> *and him alone shall you serve."*

Then he led him to Jerusalem, made him stand on the parapet of the temple, and said to him, "If you are the Son of God, throw yourself down from here, for it is written:

> *He will command his angels concerning you, to guard you,*

and:

> *With their hands they will support you,*
> *lest you dash your foot against a stone."*

Jesus said to him in reply, "It also says, *You shall not put the Lord, your God, to the test."* When the devil had finished every temptation, he departed from him for a time.

The Gospel of the Lord. **Praise to you, Lord Jesus Christ.**

Deuteronomy is a book in the Old Testament or Hebrew Scriptures. In its pages is found the belief that there is only one God, and that the people of God should be united. This name comes from the Greek word meaning "the second law" and refers to the second time that God gave the law to Moses. It was written 600 years before Christ.

The **altar** is a table or rock upon which a sacrifice was offered to God: for example, an animal, some food or incense. Today, the altar is the table upon which the priest celebrates Mass, which is also a sacrifice — of Jesus Christ — that we offer to God.

The **Arameans** were a people that lived in Syria and Mesopotamia, parts of the Middle East. They were ancestors of the Hebrews.

To **bow down** is to lie before someone, with your face on the ground, as a sign of respect, admiration and veneration. You would only do this before a person who was very important.

In the Letter to the Romans, Saint Paul writes that to be saved, we must not only have faith in Jesus as the Son of God, but we must also **confess** or say out loud what we believe. Our inward faith must be matched by outward signs in the way we live our life.

The **devil** is the one who puts temptations before us to lead us away from God. In today's gospel, the devil tempts Jesus with worldly riches and power, hoping to turn Jesus away from God and his mission, but Jesus pays no attention to the devil.

March 16
2nd Sunday of Lent

First Reading (Genesis 15:5-12, 17-18)

The Lord God took **Abram** outside and said, "Look up at the sky and count the stars, if you can. Just so," he added, "shall your descendants be." Abram put his faith in the LORD, who credited it to him as an act of righteousness.

He then said to him, "I am the LORD who brought you from Ur of the Chaldeans to give you this land as a possession." "O Lord GOD," he asked, "how am I to know that I shall possess it?" He answered him, "Bring me a three-year-old heifer, a three-year-old she-goat, a three-year-old ram, a turtledove, and a young pigeon." Abram brought him all these, split them in two, and placed each half opposite the other; but the birds he did not cut up. Birds of prey swooped down on the carcasses, but Abram stayed with them. As the sun was about to set, a trance fell upon Abram, and a deep, terrifying darkness enveloped him.

When the sun had set and it was dark, there appeared a smoking fire pot and a flaming torch, which passed between those pieces. It was on that occasion that the LORD made a covenant with Abram, saying: "To your descendants I give this land, from the Wadi of Egypt to the Great River, the **Euphrates**."

The word of the Lord. **Thanks be to God.**

Responsorial Psalm (Psalm 27:1, 7-8, 8-9, 13-14)

R. **The Lord is my light and my salvation.**

The LORD is my light and my salvation;
whom should I fear?
The LORD is my life's refuge;
of whom should I be afraid? R.

Hear, O LORD, the sound of my call;
have pity on me, and answer me.
Of you my heart speaks; you my glance seeks. R.

Your presence, O LORD, I seek.
Hide not your face from me;
do not in anger repel your servant.
You are my helper: cast me not off. R.

I believe that I shall see the bounty of the LORD
in the land of the living.
Wait for the LORD with courage;
be stouthearted, and wait for the LORD. R.

Second Reading (Philippians 3:17–4:1)

For the shorter version, omit the indented part in brackets.

[Join with others in being imitators of me, brothers and sisters, and observe those who thus conduct themselves according to the model you have in us. For many, as I have often told you and now tell you even in tears, conduct themselves as enemies of the cross of Christ. Their end is destruction. Their God is their stomach; their glory is in their "shame." Their minds are occupied with earthly things. But]

(Brothers and sisters:) Our citizenship is in heaven, and from it we also await a savior, the Lord Jesus Christ. He will change our lowly body to conform with his glorified body by the power that enables him also to bring all things into subjection to himself.

Therefore, my brothers and sisters, whom I love and long for, my joy and crown, in this way stand firm in the Lord, (beloved).

The word of the Lord. **Thanks be to God.**

Gospel (Luke 9:28b-36)

A reading from the holy Gospel according to Luke.
Glory to you, O Lord.

Jesus took **Peter, John, and James** and went up the mountain to pray. While he was praying his face changed in appearance and his clothing became dazzling white. And behold, two men were conversing with him, Moses and Elijah, who appeared in glory and spoke of his exodus that he was going to accomplish in Jerusalem. Peter and his companions had been overcome by sleep, but becoming fully awake, they saw his glory and the two men standing with him. As they were about to part from him, Peter said to Jesus, "Master, it is good that we are here; let us make three tents, one for you, one for Moses, and one for Elijah." But he did not know what he was saying. While he was still speaking, a cloud came and cast a shadow over them, and they became frightened when they entered the cloud. Then from the cloud came a voice that said, "This is my chosen Son; **listen to him**." After the voice had spoken, Jesus was found alone. They fell silent and did not at that time tell anyone what they had seen.

The Gospel of the Lord. **Praise to you, Lord Jesus Christ.**

Key Words

Genesis is the first book of the Bible. In it we find the stories of the creation of the world, the Flood, the beginning of faith in God, and many other stories showing how the Hebrew people came to understand that God loved them and asked them to love God in return.

Abram is the first man who had true faith in God. God promised him a prosperous life and many descendants, in return for being faithful and refusing to worship other gods. When Abram agreed, God gave him a new name, Abraham.

The **Euphrates** is an important river in Asia Minor that empties into the Persian Gulf. It flows through modern-day Turkey, Syria and Iraq. Together with the Tigris River, it irrigates what was once a very fertile area.

The **Philippians** were a community of Christians to whom Saint Paul wrote a friendly letter while he was in prison. Paul thanked them for sending money and encouraged them to continue to have faith in Jesus. Philippi is located in present-day northern Greece.

Peter, John, and James were three apostles, or friends of Jesus, who accompanied him in the last years of his life. Jesus chose them to be near him during important moments, such as his Transfiguration, and to be witnesses of his resurrection.

In this mysterious passage about the life of Jesus, a voice from a cloud said, **"Listen to him."** The three disciples then clearly understood that Jesus spoke with authority from God and that God wanted them to pay attention to all that Jesus taught them.

The readings for Year A may be used in place of these.

First Reading (Exodus 3:1-8a, 13-15)

Moses was tending the flock of his father-in-law Jethro, the priest of Midian. Leading the flock across the desert, he came to Horeb, the mountain of God. There an angel of the LORD appeared to Moses in fire flaming out of a bush. As he looked on, he was surprised to see that the bush, though on fire, was not consumed. So Moses decided, "I must go over to look at this remarkable sight, and see why the bush is not burned."

When the LORD saw him coming over to look at it more closely, God called out to him from the bush, "Moses! Moses!" He answered, "Here I am." God said, "Come no nearer! Remove the sandals from your feet, for the place where you stand is holy ground. I am the God of your fathers," he continued, "the God of Abraham, the God of Isaac, the God of Jacob." Moses hid his face, for he was afraid to look at God. But the LORD said, "I have witnessed the affliction of my people in Egypt and have heard their cry of complaint against their slave drivers, so I know well what they are suffering. Therefore I have come down to rescue them from the hands of the Egyptians and lead them out of that land into a good and spacious land, a land flowing with milk and honey."

Moses said to God, "But when I go to the Israelites and say to them, 'The God of your fathers has sent me to you,' if they ask me, 'What is his name?' what am I to tell them?" God replied, "I am who am." Then he added, "This is what you shall tell the Israelites: **I AM** sent me to you."

God spoke further to Moses, "Thus shall you say to the Israelites: The LORD, the God of your fathers, the God of Abraham, the God of Isaac, the God of Jacob, has sent me to you.

"This is my name forever;
    thus am I to be remembered through all generations."

The word of the Lord. **Thanks be to God.**

Responsorial Psalm (Psalm 103:1-2, 3-4, 6-7, 8, 11)

R︎. **The Lord is kind and merciful.**

Bless the LORD, O my soul;
   and all my being, bless his holy name.
Bless the LORD, O my soul,
   and forget not all his benefits. R︎.

He pardons all your iniquities,
   heals all your ills.
He redeems your life from destruction,
   crowns you with kindness and compassion. R︎.

The LORD secures justice
   and the rights of all the oppressed.
He has made known his ways to Moses,
   and his deeds to the children of Israel. R︎.

Merciful and gracious is the LORD,
   slow to anger and abounding in kindness.
For as the heavens are high above the earth,
   so surpassing is his kindness toward those
      who fear him. R︎.

Second Reading (1 Corinthians 10:1-6, 10-12)

I do not want you to be unaware, brothers and sisters, that our **ancestors** were all under the cloud and all passed through the sea, and all of them were baptized into Moses in the cloud and in the sea. All ate the same spiritual food, and all drank the same spiritual drink, for they drank from a spiritual rock that followed them, and the rock was the Christ. Yet God was not pleased with most of them, for they were struck down in the desert.

These things happened as examples for us, so that we might not **desire** evil things, as they did. Do not grumble as some of them did, and suffered death by the destroyer. These things happened to them as an example, and they have been written down as a warning to us, upon whom the end of the ages has come. Therefore, whoever thinks he is standing secure should take care not to fall.

The word of the Lord. **Thanks be to God.**

Gospel (Luke 13:1-9)

A reading from the holy Gospel according to Luke.
Glory to you, O Lord.

Some people told Jesus about the Galileans whose blood **Pilate** had mingled with the blood of their sacrifices. Jesus said to them in reply, "Do you think that because these Galileans suffered in this way they were greater sinners than all other Galileans? By no means! But I tell you, if you do not repent, you will all perish as they did! Or those eighteen people who were killed when the tower at Siloam fell on them—do you think they were more guilty than everyone else who lived in Jerusalem? By no means! But I tell you, if you do not repent, you will all perish as they did!"

And he told them this parable: "There once was a person who had a fig tree planted in his orchard, and when he came in search of fruit on it but found none, he said to the gardener, 'For three years now I have come in search of fruit on this fig tree but have found none. So cut it down. Why should it exhaust the soil?' He said to him in reply, 'Sir, leave it for this year also, and I shall cultivate the ground around it and fertilize it; it may bear fruit in the future. If not you can cut it down.' "

The Gospel of the Lord. **Praise to you, Lord Jesus Christ.**

The second book of the Bible is called **Exodus.** It is an important book because it tells how God liberated his people from slavery in Egypt, made a covenant with them, and gave them the Ten Commandments, which taught them how to live correctly. In addition to these stories, the book of Exodus outlines laws and explains how to prepare certain celebrations, such as the Passover.

The Hebrew God was known by four letters: YHWH. This name means, **"I am** who I am," taken from the verb "to be." This name shows that God is the origin of all being and the giver of life.

Saul was a Jew who persecuted the Christians. Thanks to an encounter with the risen Christ, he stopped persecuting Christians and became a follower of Jesus. His change was so radical that he even changed his name to **Paul.** Paul was a great Christian apostle. He travelled far and wide to preach the gospel. He wrote many important letters that came to form a large part of the New Testament or Christian Scriptures.

The **ancestors** Saint Paul refers to were those who left slavery in Egypt and who wandered in the desert for 40 years before coming to the Promised Land. Because they lived before the time of Christ, they did not know Jesus, but God was faithful to the covenant he had made with them.

Although God had released his people from slavery in Egypt, they grew discontented and desired to return to their old way of life. Saint Paul warns us not to make the same mistake, but to **desire** a life of faithfulness to God and his promises.

Pontius **Pilate** was the Roman governor of Judea, the southern part of Israel. This is the same Pilate who condemned Jesus to die on the cross.

March 30

4th Sunday of Lent

The readings for Year A may be used in place of these.

First Reading (Joshua 5:9a, 10-12)

The LORD said to **Joshua**, "Today I have removed the reproach of Egypt from you."

While the Israelites were encamped at Gilgal on the plains of Jericho, they celebrated the **Passover** on the evening of the fourteenth of the month. On the day after the Passover, they ate of the produce of the land in the form of **unleavened cakes** and parched grain. On that same day after the Passover, on which they ate of the produce of the land, the **manna** ceased. No longer was there manna for the Israelites, who that year ate of the yield of the land of Canaan.

The word of the Lord. **Thanks be to God.**

Responsorial Psalm (Psalm 34:2-3, 4-5, 6-7)

R. **Taste and see the goodness of the Lord.**

I will bless the LORD at all times;
    his praise shall be ever in my mouth.
Let my soul glory in the LORD;
    the lowly will hear me and be glad. R.

Glorify the LORD with me,
    let us together extol his name.
I sought the LORD, and he answered me
    and delivered me from all my fears. R.

Look to him that you may be radiant with joy,
    and your faces may not blush with shame.
When the poor one called out, the LORD heard,
    and from all his distress he saved him. R.

Second Reading (2 Corinthians 5:17-21)

Brothers and sisters: Whoever is in Christ is a new creation: the old things have passed away; behold, new things have come. And all this is from God, who has reconciled us to himself through Christ and given us the ministry of reconciliation, namely, **God was reconciling the world to himself** in Christ, not counting their trespasses against them and entrusting to us the message of reconciliation. So we are ambassadors for Christ, as if God were appealing through us. We implore you on behalf of Christ, be reconciled to God. For our sake he made him to be sin who did not know sin, so that we might become the righteousness of God in him.

The word of the Lord. **Thanks be to God.**

Gospel (Luke 15:1-3, 11-32)

A reading from the holy Gospel according to Luke. **Glory to you, O Lord.**

Tax collectors and sinners were all drawing near to listen to Jesus, but the Pharisees and scribes began to complain, saying, "This man welcomes sinners and eats with them." So to them Jesus addressed this **parable**: "A man had two sons, and the younger son said to his father, 'Father give me the share of your estate that should come to me.' So the father divided the property between them. After a few days, the younger son collected all his belongings and set off to a distant country where he squandered his inheritance on a life of dissipation. When he had freely spent everything, a severe famine struck that country, and he found himself in dire need. So he hired himself out to one of the local citizens who sent him to his farm to tend the swine. And he longed to eat his fill of the pods on which the swine fed, but nobody gave him any. Coming to his senses he thought, 'How many of my father's hired workers have more than enough food to eat, but here am I, dying from hunger. I shall get up and go to my father and I shall say to him, "Father, I have sinned against heaven and against you. I no longer deserve to be called your son; treat me as you would treat one of your hired workers." ' So he got up and went back to his father. While he was still a long way off, his father caught sight of him, and was filled with compassion. He ran to his son, embraced him and kissed him. His son said to him, 'Father, I have sinned against heaven and against you; I no longer deserve to be called your son.' But his father ordered his servants, 'Quickly bring the finest robe and put it on him; put a ring on his finger and sandals on his feet. Take the fattened calf and slaughter it. Then let us celebrate with a feast, because this son of mine was dead, and has come to life again; he was lost, and has been found.' Then the celebration began. Now the older son had been out in the field and, on his way back, as he neared the house, he heard the sound of music and dancing. He called one of the servants and asked what this might mean. The servant said to him, 'Your brother has returned and your father has slaughtered the fattened calf because he has him back safe and sound.' He became angry, and when he refused to enter the house, his father came out and pleaded with him. He said to his father in reply, 'Look, all these years I served you and not once did I disobey your orders; yet you never gave me even a young goat to feast on with my friends. But when your son returns who swallowed up your property with prostitutes, for him you slaughter the fattened calf.' He said to him, 'My son, you are here with me always; everything I have is yours. But now we must celebrate and rejoice, because your brother was dead and has come to life again; he was lost and has been found.' "

The Gospel of the Lord. **Praise to you, Lord Jesus Christ.**

When Moses died, God gave **Joshua** the responsibility of taking the people of Israel to conquer the Promised Land. The book of Joshua in the Bible tells of this conquest and how the land was divided among the twelve tribes of Israel.

The Jewish festival to celebrate the liberation of the Hebrew people from slavery is called **Passover.** It recalls how the angel of the Lord came to convince Pharaoh to let the Hebrew slaves go free. For Christians, Easter is the most important feast day, as we remember Jesus' resurrection: how he passed from death to life.

Unleavened cakes are made from wheat flour without adding yeast. This bread does not rise, resembling a crêpe or a pita. It is an important part of the Passover meal. Jesus used unleavened bread at the Last Supper because he and his disciples were having their Passover meal.

Manna is the food that God sent to the Israelites when they were crossing the desert and had nothing to eat. Manna was called "bread from heaven."

When we read that **God was reconciling the world to himself,** we understand that God forgave us and took away all the reasons he had to be angry or upset with us. God also gave the apostles the mission to reconcile everything to God and to reconcile human beings to one another. This is the vocation of everyone in the Church.

The **parable** told in today's gospel is often called The Prodigal Son. A prodigal person is someone who is extravagant and even wasteful. While the younger son is prodigal with his money, throwing it away until he has to come home because he is penniless, his father is also prodigal or extravagant with his love and forgiveness. In this parable there is both a prodigal son and a prodigal father!

April 6

5th Sunday of Lent

First Reading (Isaiah 43:16-21)

Thus says the LORD,
    who **opens a way in the sea**
    and a path in the mighty waters,
who leads out chariots and horsemen,
    a powerful army,
till they lie prostrate together, never to rise,
    snuffed out and quenched like a wick.
Remember not the events of the past,
    the things of long ago consider not;
see, I am doing something new!
    Now it springs forth, do you not perceive it?
In the desert I make a way,
    in the wasteland, rivers.
Wild beasts honor me,
    jackals and ostriches,
for I put water in the desert
    and rivers in the wasteland
    for my chosen people to drink,
the people whom I formed for myself,
    that they might announce my praise.

The word of the Lord. **Thanks be to God.**

Responsorial Psalm (Psalm 126:1-2, 2-3, 4-5, 6)

R̶. **The Lord has done great things for us;
we are filled with joy.**

When the LORD brought back the captives of **Zion**,
    we were like men dreaming.
Then our mouth was filled with laughter,
    and our tongue with rejoicing. R̶.

Then they said among the nations,
    "The LORD has done great things for them."
The LORD has done great things for us;
    we are glad indeed. R̶.

Restore our fortunes, O LORD,
    like the torrents in the southern desert.
Those that sow in tears
    shall reap rejoicing. R℣

Although they go forth weeping,
    carrying the seed to be sown,
they shall come back rejoicing,
    carrying their sheaves. R℣

Second Reading (Philippians 3:8-14)

Brothers and sisters: I consider everything as a loss because of the supreme good of knowing Christ Jesus my Lord. For his sake I have accepted the loss of all things and I consider them so much rubbish, that I may gain Christ and be found in him, not having any **righteousness** of my own based on the law but that which comes through faith in Christ, the righteousness from God, depending on faith to know him and the power of his resurrection and the sharing of his sufferings by being conformed to his death, if somehow I may attain the resurrection from the dead.

It is not that I have already taken hold of it or have already attained perfect maturity, but I continue my pursuit in hope that I may possess it, since I have indeed been taken possession of by Christ Jesus. Brothers and sisters, I for my part do not consider myself to have taken possession. Just one thing: forgetting what lies behind but straining forward to what lies ahead, I continue my pursuit toward the goal, the prize of God's upward calling, in Christ Jesus.

The word of the Lord. **Thanks be to God.**

Gospel (John 8:1-11)

A reading from the holy Gospel according to John.
Glory to you, O Lord.

Jesus went to the Mount of Olives. But early in the morning he arrived again in the temple area, and all the people started coming to him, and he sat down and taught them. Then

the scribes and the Pharisees brought a woman who had been caught in **adultery** and made her stand in the middle. They said to him, "Teacher, this woman was caught in the very act of committing adultery. Now in the law, Moses commanded us to stone such women. So what do you say?" They said this to test him, so that they could have some charge to bring against him. Jesus bent down and began to write on the ground with his finger. But when they continued asking him, he straightened up and said to them, "Let the one among you who is without sin be the first to throw a stone at her." Again he bent down and wrote on the ground. And in response, they went away one by one, beginning with the elders. So he was left alone with the woman before him. Then Jesus straightened up and said to her, "Woman, where are they? Has no one condemned you?" She replied, "No one, sir." Then Jesus said, "Neither do I condemn you. **Go, and from now on do not sin any more**."

The Gospel of the Lord. **Praise to you, Lord Jesus Christ.**

Key Words

Isaiah was a prophet who lived 800 years before Christ. His role was to help the people of Israel, especially in Jerusalem, to understand that their way of life offended God. His words moved the people to change and to have confidence in God's pardon.

. . . .

The phrase **"opens a way in the sea"** reminds us of the Israelites' crossing of the Red Sea, when God opened the waters so that the people could escape Pharaoh's army and slavery in Egypt. It shows God's great power over land and sea as well as God's care for his people.

. . . .

Zion was the name of a hill in Jerusalem where the temple was built. It is also another way of naming the city of Jerusalem, as well as the entire nation, the People of God.

. . . .

At the time of Saint Paul, a faithful Jew sought **righteousness** (or to be blameless before God) by closely obeying all God's laws and commandments.

Paul tells the Philippians that believing in Jesus Christ brings a righteousness that is freely given by God — salvation comes through faith in God and not by anything we do ourselves.

. . . .

Saint **John,** the author of the fourth Gospel, was one of the twelve apostles and Jesus loved him dearly. He accompanied Jesus in important moments, such as the Transfiguration, and he stood at the foot of the cross with Jesus' mother, Mary.

. . . .

Adultery refers to a deep breakdown in trust between a husband and a wife. To be caught in the very act of adultery means to be discovered in the moment when this trust is being broken.

. . . .

When Jesus says to the woman, **"Go, and from now on do not sin any more,"** the pardon that Jesus offers her is complete. Jesus tells her to resume her life as a new person, freed from the burden of her misdeeds.

April 13
Passion (Palm) Sunday

Gospel (Luke 19:28-40)

A reading from the holy Gospel according to Luke.
Glory to you, O Lord.

Jesus proceeded on his journey up to Jerusalem. As he drew near to Bethphage and Bethany at the place called the Mount of Olives, he sent two of his disciples. He said, "Go into the village opposite you, and as you enter it you will find a colt tethered on which no one has ever sat. Untie it and bring it here. And if anyone should ask you, 'Why are you untying it?' you will answer, 'The Master has need of it.' " So those who had been sent went off and found everything just as he had told them. And as they were untying the colt, its owners said to them, "Why are you untying this colt?" They answered, "The Master has need of it." So they brought it to Jesus, threw their cloaks over the colt, and helped Jesus to mount. As he rode along, the people were spreading their cloaks on the road; and now as he was approaching the slope of the Mount of Olives, the whole multitude of his disciples began to praise God aloud with joy for all the mighty deeds they had seen. They proclaimed:

"Blessed is the king who comes
    in the name of the Lord.
Peace in heaven
    and glory in the highest."

Some of the Pharisees in the crowd said to him, "Teacher, rebuke your disciples." He said in reply, "I tell you, if they keep silent, the stones will cry out!"

The Gospel of the Lord. **Praise to you, Lord Jesus Christ.**

First Reading (Isaiah 50:4-7)

The Lord GOD has given me
    a well-trained tongue,
that I might know how to **speak to the weary**
    a word that will rouse them.
Morning after morning
    he opens my ear that I may hear;
and I have not rebelled,
    have not turned back.
I gave my back to those who beat me,
    my cheeks to those who plucked my beard;

my face I did not shield
>from buffets and spitting.

The Lord God is my help,
>therefore I am not disgraced;
I have set my face like flint,
>knowing that I shall not be put to shame.

The word of the Lord. **Thanks be to God.**

Responsorial Psalm (Psalm 22:8-9, 17-18, 19-20, 23-24)

R̶. **My God, my God, why have you abandoned me?**

All who see me scoff at me;
>they mock me with parted lips, they wag their heads:
"He relied on the Lord; let him deliver him,
>let him rescue him, if he loves him." R̶.

Indeed, many dogs surround me,
>a pack of evildoers closes in upon me;
they have pierced my hands and my feet;
>I can count all my bones. R̶.

They divide my garments among them,
>and for my vesture they cast lots.
But you, O Lord, be not far from me;
>O my help, hasten to aid me. R̶.

I will proclaim your name to my brethren;
>in the midst of the assembly I will praise you:
"You who fear the Lord, praise him;
>all you descendants of Jacob, give glory to him;
>revere him, all you descendants of Israel!" R̶.

Second Reading (Philippians 2:6-11)

Christ Jesus, though he was in the form of God,
did not regard equality with God
>something to be grasped.
Rather, he **emptied himself**,
>taking the form of a slave,
>coming in human likeness;
>and found human in appearance,

he humbled himself,
　　becoming obedient to the point of death,
　　even death on a cross.
Because of this, God greatly exalted him
　　and bestowed on him the name
　　which is above every name,
　　that at the name of Jesus
　　every knee should bend,
　　of those in heaven and on earth and under the earth,
　　and every tongue confess that
　　Jesus Christ is Lord,
　　to the glory of God the Father.

The word of the Lord. **Thanks be to God.**

Gospel (Luke 22:14—23:56)

Several readers may proclaim the passion narrative today. (N) indicates the narrator, (†) the words of Jesus, (V) a voice, and (C) the crowd. The shorter version begins (page 145) and ends (page 148) at the asterisks.

N　The Passion of our Lord Jesus Christ according to Luke.

　　When the hour came, Jesus took his place at table with the apostles. He said to them,

†　"I have eagerly desired to eat this Passover with you before I suffer, for, I tell you, I shall not eat it again until there is fulfillment in the **kingdom of God**."

N　Then he took a cup, gave thanks, and said,

†　"Take this and share it among yourselves; for I tell you that from this time on I shall not drink of the fruit of the vine until the kingdom of God comes."

N　Then he took the bread, said the blessing, broke it, and gave it to them, saying,

†　"This is my body, which will be given for you; do this in memory of me."

N　And likewise the cup after they had eaten, saying,

†　"This cup is the new covenant in my blood, which will be shed for you.

"And yet behold, the hand of the one who is to betray me is with me on the table; for the Son of Man indeed goes as it has been determined; but woe to that man by whom he is betrayed."

N   And they began to debate among themselves who among them would do such a deed.

Then an argument broke out among them about which of them should be regarded as the greatest. He said to them,

†   "The kings of the Gentiles lord it over them and those in authority over them are addressed as 'Benefactors'; but among you it shall not be so. Rather, let the greatest among you be as the youngest, and the leader as the servant. For who is greater: the one seated at table or the one who serves? Is it not the one seated at table? I am among you as the one who serves. It is you who have stood by me in my trials; and I confer a kingdom on you, just as my Father has conferred one on me, that you may eat and drink at my table in my kingdom; and you will sit on thrones judging the twelve tribes of Israel.

"Simon, Simon, behold Satan has demanded to sift all of you like wheat, but I have prayed that your own faith may not fail; and once you have turned back, you must strengthen your brothers."

N   He said to him,

V   "Lord, I am prepared to go to prison and to die with you."

N   But he replied,

†   "I tell you, Peter, before the cock crows this day, you will deny three times that you know me."

N   He said to them,

†   "When I sent you forth without a money bag or a sack or sandals, were you in need of anything?"

C   **"No, nothing,"**

N   they replied. He said to them,

†   "But now one who has a money bag should take it, and likewise a sack, and one who does not have a sword should sell his cloak and buy one. For I tell you that this Scripture must be fulfilled in me, namely, *He was counted among the wicked*; and indeed what is written about me is coming to fulfillment."

N   Then they said,

C   **"Lord, look, there are two swords here."**

N   But he replied,

†   "It is enough!"

N   Then going out, he went, as was his custom, to the Mount of Olives, and the disciples followed him. When he arrived at the place he said to them,

†   "Pray that you may not undergo the test."

N   After withdrawing about a stone's throw from them and kneeling, he prayed, saying,

†   "Father, if you are willing, take this cup away from me; still, not my will but yours be done."

N   And to strengthen him an angel from heaven appeared to him. He was in such agony and he prayed so fervently that his sweat became like drops of blood falling on the ground. When he rose from prayer and returned to his disciples, he found them sleeping from grief. He said to them,

†   "Why are you sleeping? Get up and pray that you may not undergo the test."

N   While he was still speaking, a crowd approached and in front was one of the Twelve, a man named Judas. He went up to Jesus to kiss him. Jesus said to him,

†   "Judas, are you betraying the Son of Man with a kiss?"

N   His disciples realized what was about to happen, and they asked,

C   **"Lord, shall we strike with a sword?"**

N   And one of them struck the high priest's servant and cut off his right ear. But Jesus said in reply,

†   "Stop, no more of this!"

N   Then he touched the servant's ear and healed him. And Jesus said to the chief priests and temple guards and elders who had come for him,

†   "Have you come out as against a robber, with swords and clubs? Day after day I was with you in the temple area, and

you did not seize me; but this is your hour, the time for the **power of darkness**."

N   After arresting him they led him away and took him into the house of the high priest; Peter was following at a distance. They lit a fire in the middle of the courtyard and sat around it, and Peter sat down with them. When a maid saw him seated in the light, she looked intently at him and said,

C **"This man too was with him."**

N But he denied it saying,

V "Woman, I do not know him."

N A short while later someone else saw him and said,

C **"You too are one of them";**

N but Peter answered,

V "My friend, I am not."

N About an hour later, still another insisted,

C **"Assuredly, this man too was with him, for he also is a Galilean."**

N But Peter said,

V "My friend, I do not know what you are talking about."

N Just as he was saying this, the cock crowed, and the Lord turned and looked at Peter; and Peter remembered the word of the Lord, how he had said to him, "Before the cock crows today, you will deny me three times." He went out and began to weep bitterly. The men who held Jesus in custody were ridiculing and beating him. They blindfolded him and questioned him, saying,

C **"Prophesy! Who is it that struck you?"**

N And they reviled him in saying many other things against him.

When day came the council of elders of the people met, both chief priests and scribes, and they brought him before their Sanhedrin. They said,

C **"If you are the Christ, tell us,"**

N but he replied to them,

† "If I tell you, you will not believe, and if I question, you will not respond. But from this time on the Son of Man will be seated at the right hand of the power of God."

N They all asked,

C **"Are you then the Son of God?"**

N He replied to them,

† "You say that I am."

N Then they said,

C **"What further need have we for testimony? We have heard it from his own mouth."**

* * *

N Then the whole assembly of them (The elders of the people, chief priests and scribes,) arose and brought him before Pilate. They brought charges against him, saying,

C **"We found this man misleading our people; he opposes the payment of taxes to Caesar* and maintains that he is the Christ, a king."**

N Pilate asked him,

V "Are you the king of the Jews?"

N He said to him in reply,

† "You say so."

N Pilate then addressed the chief priests and the crowds,

V "I find this man not guilty."

N But they were adamant and said,

C **"He is inciting the people with his teaching throughout all Judea, from Galilee where he began even to here."**

N On hearing this, Pilate asked if the man was a Galilean; and upon learning that he was under Herod's jurisdiction, he sent him to Herod who was in Jerusalem at that time. Herod was very glad to see Jesus; he had been wanting to see him for a long time, for he had heard about him and had been hoping to see him perform some sign. He questioned him at length, but he gave him no answer. The chief priests and scribes, meanwhile, stood by accusing him harshly. Herod and his soldiers treated him contemptuously and mocked him, and after clothing him in resplendent garb, he sent him back to Pilate. Herod and Pilate became friends that very day, even though they had been enemies formerly. Pilate then summoned the chief priests, the rulers, and the people and said to them,

V "You brought this man to me and accused him of inciting the people to revolt. I have conducted my investigation in your presence and have not found this man guilty of the charges you have brought against him, nor did Herod, for he sent him back to us. So no capital crime has been committed by him. Therefore I shall have him flogged and then release him."

N But all together they shouted out,

C **"Away with this man! Release Barabbas* to us."**

N —Now Barabbas had been imprisoned for a rebellion that had taken place in the city and for murder.—Again Pilate addressed them, still wishing to release Jesus, but they continued their shouting,

C **"Crucify him! Crucify him!"**

N Pilate addressed them a third time,

V "What evil has this man done? I found him guilty of no capital crime. Therefore I shall have him flogged and then release him."

N With loud shouts, however, they persisted in calling for his crucifixion, and their voices prevailed. The verdict of Pilate was that their demand should be granted. So he released the man who had been imprisoned for rebellion and murder, for whom they asked, and he handed Jesus over to them to deal with as they wished.

As they led him away they took hold of a certain Simon, a Cyrenian, who was coming in from the country; and after laying the cross on him, they made him carry it behind Jesus. A large crowd of people followed Jesus, including many women who mourned and lamented him. Jesus turned to them and said,

† "Daughters of Jerusalem, do not weep for me; weep instead for yourselves and for your children for indeed, the days are coming when people will say, 'Blessed are the barren, the wombs that never bore and the breasts that never nursed.' At that time people will say to the mountains, 'Fall upon us!' and to the hills, 'Cover us!' for if these things are done when the wood is green what will happen when it is dry?"

N Now two others, both criminals, were led away with him to be executed.

When they came to the place called the Skull, they crucified him and the criminals there, one on his right, the other on his left. Then Jesus said,

† "Father, forgive them, they know not what they do."

N They divided his garments by casting lots. The people stood by and watched; the rulers, meanwhile, sneered at him and said,

C **"He saved others, let him save himself if he is the chosen one, the Christ of God."**

N Even the soldiers jeered at him. As they approached to offer him wine they called out,

C **"If you are King of the Jews, save yourself."**

N Above him there was an inscription that read, "This is the King of the Jews."

Now one of the criminals hanging there reviled Jesus, saying,

V "Are you not the Christ? Save yourself and us."

N The other, however, rebuking him, said in reply,

V "Have you no fear of God, for you are subject to the same condemnation? And indeed, we have been condemned justly, for the sentence we received corresponds to our crimes, but this man has done nothing criminal."

N Then he said,

V "Jesus, remember me when you come into your kingdom."

N He replied to him,

† "Amen, I say to you, today you will be with me in Paradise."

N   It was now about noon and darkness came over the whole land until three in the afternoon because of an eclipse of the sun. Then the veil of the temple was torn down the middle. Jesus cried out in a loud voice,

†   "Father, into your hands I commend my spirit";

N   and when he had said this he breathed his last.

(Here all kneel and pause for a short time.)

N   The centurion who witnessed what had happened glorified God and said,

V   "This man was innocent beyond doubt."

N   When all the people who had gathered for this spectacle saw what had happened, they returned home beating their breasts; but all his acquaintances stood at a distance, including the women who had followed him from Galilee and saw these events.

* * *

N   Now there was a virtuous and righteous man named Joseph who, though he was a member of the council, had not consented to their plan of action. He came from the Jewish town of Arimathea and was awaiting the kingdom of God. He went to Pilate and asked for the body of Jesus. After he had taken the body down, he wrapped it in a linen cloth and laid him in a rock-hewn tomb in which no one had yet been buried. It was the day of preparation, and the sabbath was about to begin. The women who had come from Galilee with him followed behind, and when they had seen the tomb and the way in which his body was laid in it, they returned and prepared spices and perfumed oils. Then they rested on the sabbath according to the commandment.

The Gospel of the Lord. **Praise to you, Lord Jesus Christ.**

An important task of a prophet (and also of the Church and all Christians) is to **speak to the weary** — to give strength to those who have fallen or who are weak, to offer hope to the hopeless and comfort to the lonely, and to bring consolation to those who mourn.

When we read that Christ **emptied himself**, it means that Jesus set aside his exalted or glorious condition as God in order to become a human person like us. Jesus' sacrifice was total: he gave all he was and had for our salvation.

When we come before Jesus, we realize we are in the presence of someone great and awe-inspiring. We genuflect or bow down before Jesus, because **every knee should bend** before God.

All of us should want to live in the **kingdom of God.** This will happen when all of humanity allows God's love to move us. We are called to live as children of God and love one another as sisters and brothers.

At times when it seems like evil or sin has taken over our lives or our world, it may seem that the **power of darkness** is strong. When Jesus died, his friends felt this way. However, Jesus' resurrection is proof that darkness and death have no final control over us, because Jesus conquered death.

The Romans controlled the land where Jesus lived and the people were forced to pay taxes to **Caesar**, the emperor. Although Jesus never opposed these payments, he was falsely accused of this when he was taken before the governor, Pilate.

April 20

Resurrection of the Lord
Easter Sunday

First Reading (Acts 10:34a, 37-43)

Peter proceeded to speak and said: "You know what has happened all over Judea, beginning in Galilee after the baptism that John preached, how God **anointed** Jesus of Nazareth with the Holy Spirit and power. He went about doing good and healing all those oppressed by the devil, for God was with him. We are witnesses of all that he did both in the country of the Jews and in Jerusalem. They put him to death by hanging him on a tree. **This man God raised** on the third day and granted that he be visible, not to all the people, but to us, the witnesses chosen by God in advance, who ate and drank with him after he rose from the dead. He commissioned us to preach to the people and testify that he is the one appointed by God as judge of the living and the dead. To him all the **prophets** bear witness, that everyone who believes in him will receive forgiveness of sins through his name."

The word of the Lord. **Thanks be to God.**

Responsorial Psalm (Psalm 118:1-2, 16-17, 22-23)

R. **This is the day the Lord has made;
let us rejoice and be glad.** *Or* **Alleluia.**

Give thanks to the LORD, for he is good,
for his mercy endures forever.
Let the house of Israel say,
"His mercy endures forever." R.

"The right hand of the LORD has struck with power;
the right hand of the LORD is exalted.
I shall not die, but live,
and declare the works of the LORD." R.

The stone which the builders rejected
has become the cornerstone.
By the LORD has this been done;
it is wonderful in our eyes. R.

An alternate reading follows.

Second Reading (Colossians 3:1-4)

Brothers and sisters: If then you were raised with Christ, seek **what is above**, where Christ is seated at the right hand of God. Think of what is above, not of what is **on earth**. For you have died, and your life is hidden with Christ in God. When Christ your life appears, then you too will appear with him in glory.

The word of the Lord. **Thanks be to God.**

or

Second Reading (1 Corinthians 5:6b-8)

Brothers and sisters: Do you not know that a little yeast leavens all the dough? Clear out the old yeast, so that you may become a fresh batch of dough, inasmuch as you are unleavened. For our paschal lamb, Christ, has been sacrificed. Therefore, let us celebrate the feast, not with the old yeast, the yeast of malice and wickedness, but with the unleavened bread of sincerity and truth.

The word of the Lord. **Thanks be to God.**

Sequence

Christians, to the Paschal Victim
    Offer your thankful praises!
A Lamb the sheep redeems;
    Christ, who only is sinless,
    Reconciles sinners to the Father.
Death and life have contended in that combat stupendous:
    The Prince of life, who died, reigns immortal.
Speak, Mary, declaring
    What you saw, wayfaring.
"The tomb of Christ, who is living,
    The glory of Jesus' resurrection;
Bright angels attesting,
    The shroud and napkin resting.
Yes, Christ my hope is arisen;
    To Galilee he goes before you."
Christ indeed from death is risen, our new life obtaining.
    Have mercy, victor King, ever reigning!
    Amen. Alleluia.

The gospel from the Easter Vigil, Luke 24:1-12, may also be used. Or, for an afternoon or evening Mass, Luke 24:13-35 may be used.

Gospel (John 20:1-9)

A reading from the holy Gospel according to John.
Glory to you, O Lord.

On the first day of the week, Mary of Magdala came to the tomb early in the morning, while it was still dark, and saw the stone removed from the tomb. So she ran and went to Simon Peter and to the other disciple whom Jesus loved, and told them, "They have taken the Lord from the tomb, and we don't know where they put him." So Peter and the other disciple went out and came to the tomb. They both ran, but the other disciple ran faster than Peter and arrived at the tomb first; he bent down and saw the **burial cloths** there, but did not go in. When Simon Peter arrived after him, he went into the tomb and saw the burial cloths there, and the cloth that had covered his head, not with the burial cloths but rolled up in a separate place. Then the other disciple also went in, the one who had arrived at the tomb first, and he saw and believed. For they did not yet understand the Scripture that he had to rise from the dead.

The Gospel of the Lord. **Praise to you, Lord Jesus Christ.**

Key Words

The **Acts of the Apostles** is a book in the New Testament or Christian Scriptures that describes how the Church grew after Jesus rose from the dead. It was written by Saint Luke, who also wrote one of the four gospels.

To **anoint** means to "bless with oil." In the Bible it can also mean to give someone a mission, an important job. God anoints Jesus with the Holy Spirit to show that God was giving Jesus his mission. Christians are anointed at baptism and confirmation: our mission is to live as Jesus taught us.

This man God raised: Jesus' resurrection, his passing through death to eternal life, is the most important element of the Christian faith. We believe that Jesus did not remain dead in the tomb, but overcame death, suffering, and sin. We want to live as he taught, in order to be united with him now and in the next life.

The **Prophets** were good men and women who spoke for God. Sometimes their message was harsh: they asked people to make big changes in their lives and attitudes in order to grow closer to God. At other times, they brought words of comfort.

Saint Paul wrote to the **Colossians,** a Christian community at Colossae in modern-day Turkey, to help them to understand that Jesus Christ is above everything. No powers are greater than he is.

Seeking **what is above,** that is, in heaven, includes doing the things that Jesus teaches: finding the truth, living simply, trusting in God, and caring for those in need. The things **on earth** distract us from Jesus: being selfish, hurting others, and ignoring the poor.

The **burial cloths** covered the body of a dead person in the tomb. Joseph of Arimathea and Nicodemus made sure that Jesus' body was treated with dignity and buried properly: they covered his body with linen.

April 27

2nd Sunday of Easter

First Reading (Acts 5:12-16)

Many signs and wonders were done among the people at the hands of the apostles. They were all together in **Solomon's portico**. None of the others dared to join them, but the people esteemed them. Yet more than ever, believers in the Lord, great numbers of men and women, were added to them. Thus they even carried the sick out into the streets and laid them on cots and mats so that when Peter came by, at least his shadow might fall on one or another of them. A large number of people from the towns in the vicinity of Jerusalem also gathered, bringing the sick and those disturbed by unclean spirits, and **they were all cured**.

The word of the Lord. **Thanks be to God.**

Responsorial Psalm (Psalm 118:2-4, 13-15, 22-24)

R. **Give thanks to the Lord for he is good, his love is everlasting.** *Or* **Alleluia.**

Let the house of Israel say,
    "His mercy endures forever."
Let the house of Aaron say,
    "His mercy endures forever."
Let those who fear the LORD say,
    "His mercy endures forever." R.

I was hard pressed and was falling,
    but the LORD helped me.
My strength and my courage is the LORD,
    and he has been my savior.
The joyful shout of victory
    in the tents of the just. R.

The stone which the builders rejected
    has become the cornerstone.
By the LORD has this been done;
    it is wonderful in our eyes.
This is the day the LORD has made;
    let us be glad and rejoice in it. R.

Second Reading (Revelation 1:9-11a, 12-13, 17-19)

I, John, your brother, who share with you the distress, the kingdom, and the endurance we have in Jesus, found myself on the island called Patmos because I proclaimed God's word and gave testimony to Jesus. I was **caught up in spirit** on the Lord's day and heard behind me a voice as loud as a trumpet, which said, "Write on a scroll what you see." Then I turned to see whose voice it was that spoke to me, and when I turned, I saw seven gold lampstands and in the midst of the lampstands one like a **son of man**, wearing an ankle-length robe, with a gold sash around his chest.

When I caught sight of him, I fell down at his feet as though dead. He touched me with his right hand and said, "Do not be afraid. I am the first and the last, the one who lives. Once I was dead, but now I am alive forever and ever. I hold the keys to death and the netherworld. Write down, therefore, what you have seen, and what is happening, and what will happen afterwards."

The word of the Lord. **Thanks be to God.**

Gospel (John 20:19-31)

A reading from the holy Gospel according to John.
Glory to you, O Lord.

On the evening of that first day of the week, when the doors were locked, where the disciples were, for fear of the Jews, Jesus came and stood in their midst and said to them, "Peace be with you." When he had said this, he showed them **his hands and his side**. The disciples rejoiced when they saw the Lord. Jesus said to them again, "Peace be with you. As the Father has sent me, so I send you." And when he had said this, he breathed on them and said to them, "Receive the Holy Spirit. Whose sins you forgive are forgiven them, and whose sins you retain are retained."

Thomas, called Didymus, one of the Twelve, was not with them when Jesus came. So the other disciples said to him, "We have seen the Lord." But he said to them, "Unless I see the mark of the nails in his hands and put my finger into the nailmarks and put my hand into his side, I will not believe."

Now a week later his disciples were again inside and Thomas was with them. Jesus came, although the doors were locked, and stood in their midst and said, "Peace be with you." Then he said to Thomas, "Put your finger here and see my hands, and bring your hand and put it into my side, and do not be unbelieving, but believe." Thomas answered and said to him, "My Lord and my God!" Jesus said to him, "Have you come to believe because you have seen me? Blessed are those who **have not seen and have believed**."

Now Jesus did many other signs in the presence of his disciples that are not written in this book. But these are written that you may come to believe that Jesus is the Christ, the Son of God, and that through this belief you may have life in his name.

The Gospel of the Lord. **Praise to you, Lord Jesus Christ.**

Key Words

The first reading in the Sunday Mass usually comes from the Old Testament. During the Easter season, it is taken from the New Testament book of the **Acts of the Apostles.** This book relates how God went about forming the first Christian communities after the resurrection of Jesus.

Solomon's Portico or doorway was in the great atrium of the temple in Jerusalem. It was the entrance to the area where only the Jews could be present.

There were a great number of conversions to Christianity in the first years after the resurrection. **They were all cured** is a sign of the miracles that were performed. The early Church shared in the power that Jesus showed toward people who were suffering.

Revelation is the last book of the Bible, found in the New Testament. It is written in a symbolic way. Everything has a meaning: the colors,

the numbers, the animals. These images and stories were meant to give hope to Christians who were being persecuted.

A person who experiences a strong feeling of peace when deep in prayer can be said to be **caught up in spirit.** For a few moments, this person may be deeply in God's presence.

The **"one like a son of man"** in the reading from Revelation is Jesus resurrected. Son of Man is one of the many names given to the Messiah.

By showing **his hands and his side,** Jesus presented the scars left by the nails and the lance that pierced his chest. It is a way of saying, "It's me. I was dead, but now I am alive."

When Jesus says, "Blessed are those who **have not seen and have believed,"** we can imagine he is speaking to us. Jesus walked the earth over two thousand years ago, and yet we believe in him without having seen him.

May 4

3rd Sunday of Easter

First Reading (Acts 5:27-32, 40b-41)

When the captain and the court officers had brought the apostles in and made them stand before the Sanhedrin, the high priest questioned them, "We gave you strict orders, did we not, to stop teaching in that name? Yet you have filled Jerusalem with your teaching and want to bring this man's blood upon us." But Peter and the apostles said in reply, "We must obey God rather than men. The God of our ancestors raised Jesus, though you had him killed by hanging him on a tree. God **exalted** him at his right hand as leader and savior to grant Israel repentance and forgiveness of sins. We are witnesses of these things, as is the Holy Spirit whom God has given to those who obey him."

The **Sanhedrin** ordered the apostles to stop speaking in the name of Jesus, and dismissed them. So they left the presence of the Sanhedrin, rejoicing that they had been found worthy to suffer dishonor for the sake of the name.

The word of the Lord. **Thanks be to God.**

Responsorial Psalm (Psalm 30:2, 4, 5-6, 11-12, 13)

R. **I will praise you, Lord, for you have rescued me.**
Or **Alleluia.**

I will **extol** you, O LORD, for you drew me clear
  and did not let my enemies rejoice over me.
O LORD, you brought me up from the netherworld;
  you preserved me from among those going down
    into the pit. R.

Sing praise to the LORD, you his faithful ones,
  and give thanks to his holy name.
For his anger lasts but a moment;
  a lifetime, his good will.
At nightfall, weeping enters in,
  but with the dawn, rejoicing. R.

Hear, O LORD, and have pity on me;
  O LORD, be my helper.
You changed my mourning into dancing;
  O LORD, my God, forever will I give you thanks. R.

Second Reading (Revelation 5:11-14)

I, John, looked and heard the voices of many angels who surrounded the throne and the living creatures and the elders. They were countless in number, and they cried out in a loud voice:

"Worthy is the **Lamb** that was slain
    to receive power and riches, wisdom and strength,
    honor and glory and blessing."

Then I heard every creature in heaven and on earth and under the earth and in the sea, everything in the universe, cry out:

"To the one who sits on the throne and to the Lamb
    be blessing and honor, glory and might,
    forever and ever."

The four living creatures answered, "**Amen**," and the elders fell down and worshiped.

The word of the Lord. **Thanks be to God.**

Gospel (John 21:1-19)

The shorter reading ends at the asterisks.

A reading from the holy Gospel according to John.
Glory to you, O Lord.

At that time, Jesus revealed himself again to his disciples at the Sea of Tiberias. He revealed himself in this way. Together were Simon Peter, Thomas called Didymus, Nathanael from Cana in Galilee, Zebedee's sons, and two others of his disciples. Simon Peter said to them, "I am going fishing." They said to him, "We also will come with you." So they went out and got into the boat, but that night they caught nothing. When it was already dawn, Jesus was standing on the shore; but the disciples did not realize that it was Jesus. Jesus said to them, "Children, have you caught anything to eat?" They answered him, "No." So he said to them, "Cast the net over the right side of the boat and you will find something." So they cast it, and were not able to pull it in because of the number of fish. So **the disciple whom Jesus loved** said to Peter, "It is the Lord." When Simon Peter heard that it was the Lord, he tucked in his garment, for he was lightly clad, and jumped into the sea. The other disciples came in the boat, for they were not far from shore, only about a hundred yards, dragging the net with the fish. When they climbed out on shore, they saw a charcoal fire with fish on it and bread. Jesus said to them, "Bring some of the fish you just caught." So Simon Peter went over and dragged the net ashore full of one hundred fifty-three large fish. Even though there were so many, the net was not torn. Jesus said to them, "Come, have breakfast." And none of the disciples dared to ask him, "Who are you?" because they realized it was the Lord. Jesus came over and took the bread and gave it to them, and in like manner the fish. This was now the third time Jesus was revealed to his disciples after being raised from the dead.

* * *

When they had finished breakfast, Jesus said to Simon Peter, "Simon, son of John, do you love me more than these?" Simon Peter answered him, "Yes, Lord, you know that I love you." Jesus said to him, "**Feed my lambs**." He then said to Simon Peter a second time, "Simon, son of John, do you love me?" Simon Peter answered him, "Yes, Lord, you know that I love you." Jesus said to him, "Tend my sheep." Jesus said to him the **third time**, "Simon, son of John, do you love me?" Peter was distressed that Jesus had said to him a third time, "Do you love me?" and he said to him, "Lord, you know everything; you know that I love you." Jesus said to him, "Feed my sheep. Amen, amen, I say to you, when you were younger, you used to dress yourself and go where you wanted; but when you grow old, you will stretch out your hands, and someone else will dress you and lead you where you do not want to go." He said this signifying by what kind of death he would glorify God. And when he had said this, he said to him, "Follow me."

The Gospel of the Lord.
Praise to you, Lord Jesus Christ.

Key Words

To say that God **exalted** Jesus is to say that he raised him, elevated him and resurrected him. Jesus is the first-born of all creation.

The **sanhedrin** was the most important group of Jews at the time of Jesus. It was a group of elders and wise men who discussed religious matters and who judged criminals.

When we **extol** someone, we praise them with great enthusiasm. The Psalmist has known sadness and danger in his life, but God has turned his "mourning into dancing"! For this reason, the Psalmist extols God, his power and his goodness.

The **Lamb** is a representation of Jesus. In the Jewish tradition, the people offered God a sacrifice of different animals, including both young and adult sheep. Because Jesus' sacrifice reconciled us to God, he is called the Lamb of God in the Bible.

Amen is a Hebrew word that means "yes, I agree, I promise." It is a powerful word — a word we use at the end of our prayers, to confirm that we mean what we say.

In the Gospel according to John, the apostle John who wrote the Gospel refers to himself as the **disciple whom Jesus loved.** When he was on the cross, Jesus asked this same beloved apostle to take care of Mary, his mother. John then took Mary into his own home.

When Jesus told Peter to **"feed my lambs,"** he was naming Peter to leadership of the community (today the person with this responsibility is the Pope, the successor of Peter). Jesus was also showing how this leadership was to be exercised — with the same tender care a shepherd uses to care for his sheep.

On the day that Jesus was arrested and crucified, Peter, afraid that he would also be arrested, said once, twice, and then a **third time** that he didn't know Jesus. After the resurrection, Jesus asked Peter three times if he truly loved him, and Peter responded "yes." His three denials were replaced by three acceptances.

livingwithchrist.us

May 11

4th Sunday of Easter

First Reading (Acts 13:14, 43-52)

Paul and **Barnabas** continued on from Perga and reached Antioch in Pisidia. On the sabbath they entered the synagogue and took their seats. Many Jews and worshipers who were **converts** to Judaism followed Paul and Barnabas, who spoke to them and urged them to remain faithful to the grace of God.

On the following sabbath almost the whole city gathered to hear the word of the Lord. When the Jews saw the crowds, they were filled with jealousy and with violent abuse **contradicted** what Paul said. Both Paul and Barnabas spoke out boldly and said, "It was necessary that the word of God be spoken to you first, but since you reject it and condemn yourselves as unworthy of eternal life, we now turn to the Gentiles. For so the Lord has commanded us, *I have made you a light to the Gentiles, that you may be an instrument of salvation to the ends of the earth.*"

The **Gentiles** were delighted when they heard this and glorified the word of the Lord. All who were destined for eternal life came to believe, and the word of the Lord continued to spread through the whole region. The Jews, however, incited the women of prominence who were worshipers and the leading men of the city, stirred up a persecution against Paul and Barnabas, and expelled them from their territory. So they shook the dust from their feet in protest against them, and went to Iconium. The disciples were filled with joy and the Holy Spirit.

The word of the Lord. **Thanks be to God.**

Responsorial Psalm (Psalm 100:1-2, 3, 5)

R. **We are his people, the sheep of his flock.**
Or **Alleluia.**

Sing joyfully to the LORD, all you lands;
   serve the LORD with gladness;
   come before him with joyful song. R.

Know that the LORD is God;
   he made us, his we are;
   his people, the **flock he tends**. R.

The LORD is good:
>   his kindness endures forever,
>   and his faithfulness, to all generations. R.

Second Reading (Revelation 7:9, 14b-17)

I, John, had a vision of a great multitude, which no one could count, from every nation, race, people, and tongue. They stood before the throne and before the Lamb, wearing white robes and holding **palm branches in their hands**.

Then one of the elders said to me, "These are the ones who have survived the time of great distress; they have washed their robes and made them white in the blood of the Lamb.

> "For this reason they stand before God's throne
>   and worship him day and night in his temple.
> The one who sits on the throne will shelter them.
> They will not hunger or thirst anymore,
>   nor will the sun or any heat strike them.
> For the Lamb who is in the center of the throne
>   will shepherd them
>   and lead them to springs of life-giving water,
>   and God will wipe away every tear from their eyes."

The word of the Lord. **Thanks be to God.**

Gospel (John 10:27-30)

A reading from the holy Gospel according to John.
Glory to you, O Lord.

Jesus said: "My sheep hear my voice; I know them, and they follow me. I give them eternal life, and they shall never perish. No one can take them out of my hand. My Father, who has given them to me, is greater than all, and no one can take them out of the Father's hand. The Father and I are one."

The Gospel of the Lord. **Praise to you, Lord Jesus Christ.**

Key Words

Barnabas was a generous Christian. When Saul (Saint Paul) converted to Christianity, Barnabas introduced Paul to the apostles in Jerusalem, and later traveled with Paul during his long apostolic journeys.

Converts were people who had come to believe the Christian faith, but were not yet baptized.

For some time, Christianity was not distinguished as a different religion from Judaism. Only when difficulties arose, and the Jewish officials **contradicted** Paul, did these religions separate.

Gentiles was a term that referred to all people who were not followers of the Jewish religion.

The Hebrew word **Alleluia** means "praise to God — we must give thanks!" On Easter Sunday when we celebrate the resurrection of Jesus, and throughout the Easter season, we sing and say this word often at Mass.

The Psalmist calls us the **flock he tends** to remind us that God loves and cares for us just as a shepherd loves and cares for his sheep. Nothing can separate us from the care of God.

In the book of Revelation, if someone carried **palm branches in their hands** it meant that the person would die a martyr's death. For this reason, the statues of martyrs often show the saints carrying a palm branch in their hand.

May 18
5th Sunday of Easter

First Reading (Acts 14:21-27)

After Paul and Barnabas had proclaimed the good news to that city and made a considerable number of disciples, they returned to Lystra and to Iconium and to Antioch. They strengthened the spirits of the disciples and exhorted them to persevere in the faith, saying, "It is necessary for us to undergo many hardships to enter the kingdom of God." They appointed **elders** for them in each church and, with prayer and fasting, commended them to the Lord in whom they had put their faith. Then they traveled through Pisidia and reached Pamphylia. After proclaiming the word at Perga they went down to Attalia. From there they sailed to Antioch, where they had been commended to the grace of God for the work they had now accomplished. And when they arrived, they called the church together and reported what God had done with them and how he had opened the door of faith to the Gentiles.

The word of the Lord. **Thanks be to God.**

Responsorial Psalm (Psalm 145:8-9, 10-11, 12-13)

R. **I will praise your name forever, my king and my God.**
Or **Alleluia.**

The LORD is gracious and merciful,
    slow to anger and of great kindness.
The LORD is good to all
    and compassionate toward all his works. R.

Let all your works give you thanks, O LORD,
    and let your faithful ones bless you.
Let them discourse of the glory of your kingdom
    and speak of your might. R.

Let them make known your might
        to the children of Adam,
    and the glorious splendor of your kingdom.
Your kingdom is a kingdom for all ages,
    and your dominion endures through
        all generations. R.

Second Reading (Revelation 21:1-5a)

Then I, John, saw a new heaven and a new earth. The former heaven and the former earth had passed away, and the sea was no more. I also saw the holy city, a **new Jerusalem**, coming down out of heaven from God, prepared as a bride adorned for her husband. I heard a loud voice from the throne saying, "Behold, God's dwelling is with the human race. He will dwell with them and they will be his people and God himself will always be with them as their God. He will wipe every tear from their eyes, and there shall be no more death or mourning, wailing or pain, for the old order has passed away."

The One who sat on the throne said, "Behold, I make all things new."

The word of the Lord.
Thanks be to God.

Gospel (John 13:31-33a, 34-35)

A reading from the holy Gospel according to John.
Glory to you, O Lord.

When Judas had left them, Jesus said, "Now is the Son of Man **glorified**, and God is glorified in him. If God is glorified in him, God will also glorify him in himself, and God will glorify him at once. My children, I will be with you **only a little while longer**. I give you a **new commandment**: love one another. As I have loved you, so you also should love one another. This is how **all will know** that you are my disciples, if you have love for one another."

The Gospel of the Lord. **Praise to you, Lord Jesus Christ.**

Key Words

The apostles looked for wise men or **elders** to help strengthen the faith life of the Christian communities. In today's Church, the priests collaborate with the bishops to play this role.

The book of Revelation speaks of the Church as the **new Jerusalem,** the new people of God, the new kingdom of peace.

Because he knew what lay before him, Jesus was able to say that he would be **glorified.** Jesus' suffering and then his death were not the end. His resurrection and triumph over death opened the way for us to enter into heaven.

The Last Supper, where Jesus met with his disciples to celebrate the Passover, is when he tells them that he will be with them **only a little while longer**. Jesus washed his friends' feet, and, in breaking bread and sharing wine, he left us the Eucharist — his presence that we still celebrate today.

Through Moses, God gave us the Ten Commandments. Without changing these, God gave us a **new commandment** through Jesus. This most important commandment is to love one another as Jesus loved us.

Jesus desires that **all will know** who Christians are by the way we love one another. Not by our clothes, or our names, but by the way we live. This is our daily challenge!

First Reading (Acts 15:1-2, 22-29)

Some who had come down from Judea were instructing the brothers, "Unless you are circumcised according to the Mosaic practice, you cannot be saved." Because there arose no little **dissension** and debate by Paul and Barnabas with them, it was decided that Paul, Barnabas, and some of the others should go up to Jerusalem to the apostles and elders about this question.

The apostles and elders, in agreement with the whole church, decided to choose representatives and to send them to Antioch with Paul and Barnabas. The ones chosen were Judas, who was called Barsabbas, and Silas, leaders among the brothers. This is the letter delivered by them:

"The apostles and the elders, your brothers, to the brothers in Antioch, Syria, and Cilicia of Gentile origin: greetings. Since we have heard that some of our number who went out without any mandate from us have upset you with their teachings and disturbed your peace of mind, we have with one accord decided to choose representatives and to send them to you along with our beloved Barnabas and Paul, who have dedicated their lives to the name of our Lord Jesus Christ. So we are sending Judas and Silas who will also convey this same message by word of mouth: 'It is the decision of the Holy Spirit and of us not to place on you any **burden** beyond these necessities, namely, to abstain from meat sacrificed to idols, from blood, from meats of strangled animals, and from unlawful marriage. If you keep free of these, you will be doing what is right. Farewell.' "

The word of the Lord.
Thanks be to God.

Responsorial Psalm (Psalm 67:2-3, 5, 6, 8)

R. **O God, let all the nations praise you!** *Or* **Alleluia.**

May God have pity on us and bless us;
    may he let his face shine upon us.
So may your way be known upon earth;
    among all nations, your salvation. R.

May the nations be glad and exult
    because you rule the peoples in equity;
    the nations on the earth you guide. R.

May the peoples praise you, O God;
    may all the peoples praise you!
May God bless us,
    and may all the ends of the earth fear him! R.

Second Reading (Revelation 21:10-14, 22-23)

The angel took me in spirit to a great, high mountain and showed me the **holy city Jerusalem** coming down out of heaven from God. It gleamed with the splendor of God. Its radiance was like that of a precious stone, like jasper, clear as crystal. It had a massive, high wall, with twelve gates where twelve angels were stationed and on which names were inscribed, the names of the **twelve tribes** of the Israelites. There were three gates facing east, three north, three south, and three west. The wall of the city had twelve courses of stones as its foundation, on which were inscribed the twelve names of the **twelve apostles** of the Lamb.

I saw no temple in the city for its temple is the Lord God almighty and the Lamb. The city had no need of sun or moon to shine on it, for the glory of God gave it light, and its lamp was the Lamb.

The word of the Lord. **Thanks be to God.**

Gospel (John 14:23-29)

A reading from the holy Gospel according to John.
Glory to you, O Lord.

Jesus said to his disciples: "Whoever loves me will keep my word, and my Father will love him, and we will come to him and **make our dwelling with him**. Whoever does not love me does not keep my words; yet the word you hear is not mine but that of the Father who sent me.

"I have told you this while I am with you. The Advocate, the **Holy Spirit**, whom the Father will send in my name, will teach you everything and remind you of all that I told you. Peace I leave with you; my peace I give to you. Not as the world gives do I give it to you. Do not let your hearts be troubled or afraid. You heard me tell you, 'I am going away and I will come back to you.' If you loved me, you would rejoice that I am going to the Father; for the Father is greater than I. And now I have told you this before it happens, so that when it happens you may believe."

The Gospel of the Lord. **Praise to you, Lord Jesus Christ.**

Key Words

The **dissension** in the early Church was a disagreement over whether people who were not followers of the Jewish law could become Christians. Paul and Barnabas felt that God's love was available to all through membership in the Christian community, and that new Christians did not need to become Jewish first.

In the Acts of the Apostles, we read about the disciples trying to decide whether non-Jewish followers of Jesus had to follow all the Jewish laws in order to join the Church. In the end, after much discussion, the Holy Spirit led them to decide to ease the **burden** or heavy load for new followers by settling on a few laws.

The writer of the book of Revelation saw the **holy city Jerusalem** as resplendently beautiful because its people had been united to God by following Jesus and his teachings.

When the book of Revelation speaks of the **twelve tribes** of Israel, it means the whole history of these people until Jesus came. When it speaks of the **twelve apostles,** it refers to all that happened in the life of the Christian Church. So here the number twelve means all the Old Testament or Hebrew Scriptures and all the New Testament or Christian Scriptures.

When Jesus and his Father find a person who lives a holy life, they say they will **make our dwelling with them.** God will remain close to the person who loves God, so close that God dwells right within them.

After Jesus ascended to heaven, the Church had the power to carry on. The words of Jesus will not be forgotten because the **Holy Spirit** will help us remember all that Jesus taught and give us the strength to live faithfully.

June 1

Ascension of the Lord
Or *The Seventh Sunday of Easter*

*If your diocese celebrates the Ascension of the Lord on Thursday, May 29,
then this Sunday is the Seventh Sunday of Easter. The readings for the
Seventh Sunday of Easter can be found on page 182.*

First Reading (Acts 1:1-11)

In the **first book**, Theophilus, I dealt with all that Jesus did and taught until the day he was taken up, after giving instructions through the Holy Spirit to the apostles whom he had chosen. He presented himself alive to them by many proofs after he had suffered, appearing to them during forty days and speaking about the kingdom of God. While meeting with them, he enjoined them not to depart from Jerusalem, but to wait for "the promise of the Father about which you have heard me speak; for John baptized with water, but in a few days you will be baptized with the Holy Spirit."

When they had gathered together they asked him, "Lord, are you at this time going to restore the **kingdom** to Israel?" He answered them, "It is not for you to know the times or seasons that the Father has established by his own authority. But you will receive power when the Holy Spirit comes upon you, and you will be my witnesses in Jerusalem, throughout Judea and Samaria, and to the ends of the earth." When he had said this, as they were looking on, he was **lifted up**, and a cloud took him from their sight. While they were looking intently at the sky as he was going, suddenly two men dressed in white garments stood beside them. They said, "Men of Galilee, why are you standing there looking at the sky? This Jesus who has been taken up from you into heaven will return in the same way you have seen him going into heaven."

The word of the Lord. **Thanks be to God.**

Responsorial Psalm (Psalm 47:2-3, 6-7, 8-9)

R. **God mounts his throne to shouts of joy: a blare of trumpets for the Lord.** *Or* **Alleluia.**

All you peoples, clap your hands,
    shout to God with cries of gladness,
for the LORD, the Most High, the awesome,
    is the great king over all the earth. R.

God mounts his throne amid shouts of joy;
the LORD, amid trumpet blasts.
Sing praise to God, sing praise;
sing praise to our king, sing praise. R⫶

For king of all the earth is God;
sing hymns of praise.
God reigns over the nations,
God sits upon his holy throne. R⫶

An alternate reading follows.

Second Reading (Ephesians 1:17-23)

Brothers and sisters: May the God of our Lord Jesus Christ, the Father of glory, give you a Spirit of wisdom and revelation resulting in knowledge of him. May the eyes of your hearts be enlightened, that you may know what is the hope that belongs to his call, what are the riches of glory in his inheritance among the holy ones, and what is the surpassing greatness of his power for us who believe, in accord with the exercise of his great might: which he worked in Christ, raising him from the dead and seating him at his right hand in the heavens, far above every principality, authority, power, and dominion, and every name that is named not only in this age but also in the one to come. And he put all things beneath his feet and gave him as head over all things to the church, which is his body, the fullness of the one who fills all things in every way.

The word of the Lord. **Thanks be to God.**

or

Second Reading (Hebrews 9:24-28; 10:19-23)

Christ did not enter into a **sanctuary** made by hands, a copy of the true one, but heaven itself, that he might now appear before God on our behalf. Not that he might offer himself repeatedly, as the high priest enters each year into the sanctuary with blood that is not his own; if that were so, he would have had to suffer repeatedly from the foundation of the world. But now once for all he has appeared at the end of the ages to take away sin by his sacrifice. Just as it is appointed that men and women die once, and after this the judgment, so also Christ, offered once to take away the sins of many, will appear a second time, not to take away sin but to bring salvation to those who eagerly await him.

Therefore, brothers and sisters, since through the blood of Jesus we have confidence of entrance into the sanctuary by the new and living way he opened for us through the veil, that is, his flesh, and since we have "a great priest over the house of God," let us approach with a sincere heart and in absolute trust, with our hearts sprinkled clean from an evil conscience and our bodies washed in pure water. Let us hold unwaveringly to our **confession that gives us hope**, for he who made the promise is trustworthy.

The word of the Lord. **Thanks be to God.**

Gospel (Luke 24:46-53)

A reading from the holy Gospel according to Luke.
Glory to you, O Lord.

Jesus said to his disciples: "Thus it is written that the Christ would suffer and rise from the dead on the third day and that repentance, for the forgiveness of sins, would be preached in his name to all the nations, beginning from Jerusalem. You are **witnesses** of these things. And behold I am sending the promise of my Father upon you; but stay in the city until you are clothed with power from on high."

Then he led them out as far as Bethany, raised his hands, and blessed them. As he blessed them he parted from them and was taken up to heaven. They did him homage and then returned to Jerusalem with great joy, and they were continually in the temple praising God.

The Gospel of the Lord. **Praise to you, Lord Jesus Christ.**

The Seventh Sunday of Easter

First Reading (Acts 7:55-60)

Stephen, filled with the Holy Spirit, looked up intently to heaven and saw the glory of God and Jesus standing at the right hand of God, and Stephen said, "Behold, I see the heavens opened and the Son of Man standing at the right hand of God." But they cried out in a loud voice, covered their ears, and rushed upon him together. They threw him out of the city, and began to stone him. The witnesses laid down their cloaks at the feet of a young man named Saul. As they were stoning Stephen, he called out, "Lord Jesus, receive my spirit." Then he fell to his knees and cried out in a loud voice, "Lord, do not hold this sin against them"; and when he said this, he fell asleep.

The word of the Lord. **Thanks be to God.**

Responsorial Psalm (Psalm 97:1-2, 6-7, 9)

R̶. **The Lord is king, the most high over all the earth.**
Or **Alleluia.**

The LORD is king; let the earth rejoice;
    let the many islands be glad.
Justice and judgment are the foundation of his throne. R̶.

The heavens proclaim his justice,
    and all peoples see his glory.
All gods are prostrate before him. R̶.

You, O LORD, are the Most High over all the earth,
    exalted far above all gods. R̶.

Second Reading (Revelation 22:12-14, 16-17, 20)

I, John, heard a voice saying to me: "Behold, I am coming soon. I bring with me the recompense I will give to each according to his deeds. I am the Alpha and the Omega, the first and the last, the beginning and the end."

Blessed are they who wash their robes so as to have the right to the tree of life and enter the city through its gates.

"I, Jesus, sent my angel to give you this testimony for the churches. I am the root and offspring of David, the bright morning star."

The Spirit and the bride say, "Come." Let the hearer say, "Come." Let the one who thirsts come forward, and the one who wants it receive the gift of life-giving water.

The one who gives this testimony says, "Yes, I am coming soon." Amen! Come, Lord Jesus!

The word of the Lord. **Thanks be to God.**

Gospel (John 17:20-26)

A reading from the holy Gospel according to John.
Glory to you, O Lord.

Lifting up his eyes to heaven, Jesus prayed, saying: "Holy Father, I pray not only for them, but also for those who will believe in me through their word, so that they may all be one, as you, Father, are in me and I in you, that they also may be in us, that the world may believe that you sent me. And I have given them the glory you gave me, so that they may be one, as we are one, I in them and you in me, that they may be brought to perfection as one, that the world may know that you sent me, and that you loved them even as you loved me. Father, they are your gift to me. I wish that where I am they also may be with me, that they may see my glory that you gave me, because you loved me before the foundation of the world. Righteous Father, the world also does not know you, but I know you, and they know that you sent me. I made known to them your name and I will make it known, that the love with which you loved me may be in them and I in them."

The Gospel of the Lord. **Praise to you, Lord Jesus Christ.**

Key Words

Saint Luke, the author of the Acts of the Apostles, also wrote a gospel. The **first book** he refers to here is that gospel. The Gospel of Luke tells us what Jesus did, what he taught, and how he died and rose from the dead. The second book, the Acts of the Apostles, describes the first years of the life of the Church and the early Christian communities.

In the Bible, the expression **"kingdom** of God" describes a way of living as God asks. To enter into the kingdom means to live as children of God. The disciples, however, thought that Jesus was going to restore the independence of the Jews, releasing them from the Roman kingdom and setting up an earthly kingdom for the Jewish people.

The Ascension of the Lord celebrates the day when Christ was **lifted up** to heaven, 40 days after his resurrection. Jesus is still with us in spirit, but his resurrected body is with God.

A **sanctuary** made by human hands is a holy place of safety and rest. In some religions, only very holy people and priests can enter the sanctuary of a church or temple. Jesus entered the holiest of sanctuaries, heaven itself.

The **confession that gives us hope** is our faith in Jesus, especially our hope that he calls us to live with him in the kingdom of heaven, to enjoy everlasting life.

After the Resurrection and Ascension, the principal mission of the apostles was to be **witnesses** of the death and resurrection of Jesus. This remains the task of the followers of Christ today.

June 8
Pentecost Sunday

First Reading (Acts 2:1-11)

When the time for **Pentecost** was fulfilled, they were all in one place together. And suddenly there came from the sky a noise like a strong driving wind, and it filled the entire house in which they were. Then there appeared to them tongues as of fire, which parted and came to rest on each one of them. And they were all filled with the **Holy Spirit** and began to speak in different tongues, as the Spirit enabled them to proclaim.

Now there were devout Jews from every nation under heaven staying in Jerusalem. At this sound, they gathered in a large crowd, but they were confused because each one heard them speaking in his own language. They were astounded, and in amazement they asked, "Are not all these people who are speaking Galileans? Then how does each of us hear them in his native language? We are Parthians, Medes, and Elamites, inhabitants of Mesopotamia, Judea and Cappadocia, Pontus and Asia, Phrygia and Pamphylia, Egypt and the districts of Libya near Cyrene, as well as travelers from Rome, both Jews and converts to Judaism, Cretans and Arabs, yet we hear them speaking in our own tongues of the mighty acts of God."

The word of the Lord. **Thanks be to God.**

Responsorial Psalm (Psalm 104:1, 24, 29-30, 31, 34)

R. **Lord, send out your Spirit, and renew the face of the earth.** Or **Alleluia.**

Bless the LORD, O my soul!
O LORD, my God, you are great indeed!
How manifold are your works, O LORD!
The earth is full of your creatures. R.

If you take away their breath, they perish
and return to their dust.
When you send forth your spirit, they are created,
and you renew the face of the earth. R.

> May the glory of the Lord endure forever;
>   may the LORD be glad in his works!
> Pleasing to him be my theme;
>   I will be glad in the LORD. R.

An alternate reading follows.

Second Reading (1 Corinthians 12:3b-7, 12-13)

Brothers and sisters: No one can say, "Jesus is Lord," except by the Holy Spirit.

There are different kinds of spiritual gifts but the same Spirit; there are different forms of service but the same Lord; there are different workings but the same God who produces all of them in everyone. To each individual the manifestation of the Spirit is given for some benefit.

As a body is one though it has many parts, and all the parts of the body, though many, are one body, so also Christ. For in one Spirit we were all baptized into one body, whether Jews or Greeks, slaves or free persons, and we were all given to drink of one Spirit.

The word of the Lord. **Thanks be to God.**

Or

Second Reading (Romans 8:8-17)

Brothers and sisters: Those who are **in the flesh** cannot please God. But you are not in the flesh; on the contrary, you are **in the spirit**, if only the Spirit of God dwells in you. Whoever does not have the Spirit of Christ does not belong to him. But if Christ is in you, although the body is dead because of sin, the spirit is alive because of righteousness. If the Spirit of the one who raised Jesus from the dead dwells in you, the one who raised Christ from the dead will give life to your mortal bodies also, through his Spirit that dwells in you. Consequently, brothers and sisters, we are not debtors to the flesh, to live according to the flesh. For if you live according to the flesh, you will die, but if by the Spirit you put to death the deeds of the body, you will live.

For those who are led by the Spirit of God are sons of God. For you did not receive a spirit of slavery to fall back into fear, but you received a Spirit of adoption, through whom we cry, "Abba, Father!" The Spirit himself bears witness with our spirit that we are **children of God**, and if children, then heirs, heirs of God and joint heirs with Christ, if only we suffer with him so that we may also be glorified with him.

The word of the Lord. **Thanks be to God.**

Sequence (Veni, Sancte Spiritus)

Come, Holy Spirit, come!
And from your celestial home
    Shed a ray of light divine!
Come, Father of the poor!
Come, source of all our store!
    Come, within our bosoms shine.
You, of comforters the best;
You, the soul's most welcome guest;
    Sweet refreshment here below.
In our labor, rest most sweet;
Grateful coolness in the heat;
    Solace in the midst of woe.
O most blessed Light divine,
Shine within these hearts of yours,
    And our inmost being fill!
Where you are not, we have naught,
Nothing good in deed or thought,
    Nothing free from taint of ill.
Heal our wounds, our strength renew;
On our dryness pour your dew;
    Wash the stains of guilt away.
Bend the stubborn heart and will;
Melt the frozen, warm the chill;
    Guide the steps that go astray.
On the faithful, who adore
And confess you, evermore
    In your sevenfold gift descend.
Give them virtue's sure reward;
Give them your salvation, Lord;
    Give them joys that never end. Amen.
    Alleluia.

An alternate reading follows.

Gospel (John 20:19-23)

A reading from the holy Gospel according to John.
Glory to you, O Lord.

On the evening of that first day of the week, when the doors were locked, where the disciples were, for fear of the Jews, Jesus came and stood in their midst and said to them, "Peace be with you." When he had said this, he showed them **his hands** and **his side**. The disciples rejoiced when they saw the Lord. Jesus said to them again, "Peace be with you. As the Father has sent me, so I send you." And when he had said this, he breathed on them and said to them, "Receive the Holy Spirit. Whose sins you forgive are forgiven them, and whose sins you retain are retained."

The Gospel of the Lord. **Praise to you, Lord Jesus Christ.**

Or

Gospel (John 14:15-16, 23b-26)

A reading from the holy Gospel according to John.
Glory to you, O Lord.

Jesus said to his disciples: "If you love me, you will keep my commandments. And I will ask the Father, and he will give you another Advocate to be with you always.

"Whoever loves me will keep my word, and my Father will love him, and we will come to him and make our dwelling with him. Those who do not love me do not keep my words; yet the word you hear is not mine but that of the Father who sent me.

"I have told you this while I am with you. The **Advocate**, the Holy Spirit whom the Father will send in my name, will teach you everything and remind you of all that I told you."

The Gospel of the Lord. **Praise to you, Lord Jesus Christ.**

Key Words

Pentecost is the Greek word for a Jewish festival that takes place on the fiftieth day after Passover. Fifty days after Jesus' resurrection, the Holy Spirit descended upon all those present in the upper room of a house. For Christians, Pentecost is the feast of the coming of the Holy Spirit and the birthday of the Church.

The **Holy Spirit,** the third person of the Trinity, is always with the Church in order to help us live better. We receive the Holy Spirit in baptism as God's great gift.

When we live **in the flesh,** we live in a way totally opposite to living **in the Spirit.** To live in the flesh is to make comfort, ease, and wealth our priority. To live in the Spirit is to follow Jesus and love our neighbor as ourselves.

Christians know that we are **children of God.** If God is our parent, then all other human beings must be our brothers and sisters.

After Jesus was crucified, the disciples were sad and afraid, for they believed Jesus to be dead. To prove he was alive, Jesus showed them the wounds from his crucifixion, made by the nails in **his hands** and a spear in **his side.**

The **Advocate** is another name for the Holy Spirit, sent by Jesus to be our helper and guide until the end of time.

June 15
Solemnity of the Most Holy Trinity

First Reading (Proverbs 8:22-31)

Thus says the wisdom of God:
"The LORD possessed me, the beginning of his ways,
　　the forerunner of his prodigies of long ago;
from of old I was poured forth,
　　at the first, before the earth.
When there were no depths I was brought forth,
　　when there were no fountains or springs of water;
before the mountains were settled into place,
　　before the hills, I was brought forth;
while as yet the earth and fields were not made,
　　nor the first clods of the world.

"When the Lord established the heavens I was there,
　　when he marked out the vault over the face of the deep;
when he made firm the skies above,
　　when he fixed fast the foundations of the earth;
when he set for the sea its limit,
　　so that the waters should not transgress his command;
then was I beside him as his craftsman,
　　and I was his delight day by day,
playing before him all the while,
　　playing on the surface of his earth;
　　and I found delight in the human race."

The word of the Lord. **Thanks be to God.**

Responsorial Psalm (Psalm 8:4-5, 6-7, 8-9)

R. **O Lord, our God, how wonderful your name in all the earth!**

When I behold your heavens, the work of your fingers,
　　the moon and the stars which you set in place—
What is man that you should be mindful of him,
　　or the son of man that you should care for him? R.

You have made him little less than the angels,
　　and crowned him with glory and honor.
You have given him rule over the works of your hands,
　　putting all things under his feet: R.

All sheep and oxen,
    yes, and the beasts of the field,
The birds of the air, the fishes of the sea,
    and whatever swims the paths of the seas. R.

Second Reading (Romans 5:1-5)

Brothers and sisters: Therefore, since we have been justified by faith, we have peace with God through our Lord Jesus Christ, through whom we have gained access by faith to this grace in which we stand, and we **boast** in hope of the glory of God. Not only that, but we even boast of our afflictions, knowing that affliction produces endurance, and endurance, proven character, and proven character, hope, and hope does not disappoint, because the love of God has been poured out into our hearts through the Holy Spirit that has been given to us.

The word of the Lord. **Thanks be to God.**

Gospel (John 16:12-15)

A reading from the holy Gospel according to John.
Glory to you, O Lord.

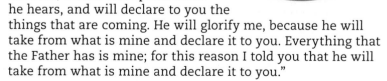

Jesus said to his disciples: "I have much more to tell you, but you cannot **bear** it now. But when he comes, the **Spirit of truth**, he will guide you to all truth. He will not speak on his own, but he will speak what he hears, and will declare to you the things that are coming. He will glorify me, because he will take from what is mine and declare it to you. Everything that the Father has is mine; for this reason I told you that he will take from what is mine and declare it to you."

The Gospel of the Lord. **Praise to you, Lord Jesus Christ.**

Key Words

The book of **Proverbs** is found in the Old Testament. A single author did not write this book. These popular sayings and expressions of knowledge were assembled over many centuries. It could be said that the author is the whole people inspired by God.

. . . .

The **Letter of Saint Paul to the Romans** is the longest letter that Saint Paul wrote. The Christians who lived in Rome belonged to a small community. Paul planned to travel to preach in Spain, and to stop on the way in Rome to visit the Christians. He sent them this letter to introduce himself, to encourage them and to remind them of the teachings of Jesus.

If we have real faith, we can **boast** of or take pride in even the most intense sufferings, because through them we come to experience a greater closeness to God.

. . . .

Jesus spent much time teaching about the kingdom of God (by his words, his miracles, and above all through his death and resurrection.) But when he was ready to say goodbye to his disciples, he realized that they had not understood, or could not **bear** to understand, everything Jesus had to tell them. The same thing happens to us: we need continually to try to understand the teachings of Jesus.

. . . .

The **Spirit of truth** is the Holy Spirit, present and working in the Church so that we may better understand and remember all that Jesus taught.

June 22
Solemnity of the Most Holy Body and Blood of Christ

First Reading (Genesis 14:18-20)

In those days, **Melchizedek**, king of Salem, brought out bread and wine, and being a priest of God Most High, he blessed Abram with these words:

> "Blessed be Abram by God Most High,
>   the creator of heaven and earth;
> and blessed be God Most High,
>   who delivered your foes into your hand."

Then Abram gave him a tenth of everything.

The word of the Lord. **Thanks be to God.**

Responsorial Psalm (Psalm 110:1, 2, 3, 4)

R. **You are a priest forever, in the line of Melchizedek.**

> The LORD said to my Lord: "Sit at my right hand
>   till I make your enemies your footstool." R.

> The scepter of your power the LORD will stretch
>   forth from Zion:
>   "Rule in the midst of your enemies." R.

> "Yours is princely power in the day of your birth,
>   in holy splendor;
> before the daystar, like the dew, I have
>   begotten you." R.

> **The** LORD **has sworn**, and he will not repent:
>   "You are a priest forever, according to the order
>   of Melchizedek." R.

Second Reading (1 Corinthians 11:23-26)

Brothers and sisters: I received from the Lord what I also handed on to you, that the Lord Jesus, on the night he was handed over, took bread, and, after he had given thanks, broke it and said, "This is my body that is for you. Do this in remembrance of me." In the same way also the cup, after supper, saying, "This cup is the new covenant in my blood. Do this, as often as you drink it, **in remembrance** of me." For as often as you eat this bread and drink the cup, you proclaim the death of the Lord until he comes.

The word of the Lord. **Thanks be to God.**

Sequence

The shorter version begins at the asterisks.

Laud, O Zion, your salvation,
Laud with hymns of exultation,
    Christ, your king and shepherd true:

Bring him all the praise you know,
He is more than you bestow.
    Never can you reach his due.

Special theme for glad thanksgiving
Is the quick'ning and the living
    Bread today before you set:

From his hands of old partaken,
As we know, by faith unshaken,
    Where the Twelve at supper met.

Full and clear ring out your chanting,
Joy nor sweetest grace be wanting,
    From your heart let praises burst:

For today the feast is holden,
When the institution olden
    Of that supper was rehearsed.

Here the new law's new oblation,
By the new king's revelation,
    Ends the form of ancient rite:

Now the new the old effaces,
Truth away the shadow chases,
    Light dispels the gloom of night.

What he did at supper seated,
Christ ordained to be repeated,
    His memorial ne'er to cease:

And his rule for guidance taking,
Bread and wine we hallow, making
    Thus our sacrifice of peace.

This the truth each Christian learns,
Bread into his flesh he turns,
    To his precious blood the wine:

Sight has fail'd, nor thought conceives,
But a dauntless faith believes,
    Resting on a pow'r divine.

Here beneath these signs are hidden
Priceless things to sense forbidden;
    Sign, not things are all we see:

Blood is poured and flesh is broken,
Yet in either wondrous token
    Christ entire we know to be.

Whoso of this food partakes,
Does not rend the Lord nor breaks;
    Christ is whole to all that tastes:

Thousands are, as one, receivers,
One, as thousands of believers,
    Eats of him who cannot waste.

Bad and good the feast are sharing,
Of what divers dooms preparing,
    Endless death, or endless life.

Life to these, to those damnation,
See how like participation
    Is with unlike issues rife.

When the sacrament is broken,
Doubt not, but believe 'tis spoken,
    That each sever'd outward token
        doth the very whole contain.

Nought the precious gift divides,
Breaking but the sign betides
    Jesus still the same abides,
        still unbroken does remain.

* * *

The shorter form of the sequence begins here.

Lo! the angel's food is given
To the pilgrim who has striven;

See the children's bread from heaven,
which on dogs may not be spent.

Truth the ancient types fulfilling,
Isaac bound, a victim willing,
Paschal lamb, its lifeblood spilling,
manna to the fathers sent.

Very bread, good shepherd, tend us,
Jesu, of your love befriend us,
You refresh us, you defend us,
Your eternal goodness send us
In the land of life to see.

You who all things can and know,
Who on earth such food bestow,
Grant us with your saints, though lowest,
Where the heav'nly feast you show,
Fellow heirs and guests to be. Amen. Alleluia.

Gospel (Luke 9:11b-17)

A reading from the holy Gospel according to Luke.
Glory to you, O Lord.

Jesus spoke to the crowds about the kingdom of God, and he healed those who needed to be cured. As the day was drawing to a close, the Twelve approached him and said, "Dismiss the crowd so that they can go to the surrounding villages and farms and find **lodging** and provisions; for we are in a deserted place here." He said to them, "Give them some food yourselves." They replied, "Five loaves and two fish are all we have, unless we ourselves go and buy food for all these people." Now the **men there numbered about five thousand**. Then he said to his disciples, "Have them sit down in groups of about fifty." They did so and made them all sit down. Then taking the five loaves and the two fish, and looking up to heaven, he said the blessing over them, broke them, and gave them to the disciples to set before the crowd. They all ate and were satisfied. And when the leftover fragments were picked up, they filled twelve wicker baskets.

The Gospel of the Lord. **Praise to you, Lord Jesus Christ.**

Key Words

The Solemnity of the **Most Holy Body and Blood of Christ** is also known by its Latin name, Corpus Christi (meaning the Body of Christ). On this day, Mass may be followed by a procession and adoration of the Blessed Sacrament.

Melchizedek was a holy man, a priest, and a king who lived long before the time of Jesus. The fact that he worshiped God by taking bread and wine, exactly as Jesus did at the Last Supper, and as we do at the Eucharist today, shows how long God has been patiently trying to show us how to live and how to pray.

When we read that **the Lord has sworn,** we understand that God has made a promise that will never be broken. Even when we turn away from God, God always keeps his promise.

When we do something **in remembrance** of someone, we are performing an action to show our respect and affection for the person who has died.

A **lodging** is a place to sleep over somewhere that is not your own house. It would be next to impossible for five thousand people or more to find lodging on such short notice.

Jesus and the disciples fed an enormous crowd, for there were surely women and children present, in addition to the **five thousand men** mentioned by Saint Luke in the gospel.

June 29
Saints Peter and Paul

First Reading (Acts 12:1-11)

In those days, King **Herod** laid hands upon some members
     of the Church to harm them.
He had James, the brother of John, killed by the sword,
    and when he saw that this was pleasing to the Jews
    he proceeded to arrest Peter also.
—It was the feast of Unleavened Bread.—
He had him taken into custody and put in prison
    under the guard of four squads of four soldiers each.
He intended to bring him before the people after Passover.
Peter thus was being kept in prison,
    but prayer by the Church was fervently being made
    to God on his behalf.

On the very night before Herod was to bring him to trial,
    Peter, secured by double chains,
    was sleeping between two soldiers,
    while outside the door guards kept watch on the prison.
Suddenly the angel of the Lord stood by him,
    and a light shone in the cell.
He tapped Peter on the side and awakened him, saying,
    "Get up quickly."
The chains fell from his wrists.
The angel said to him, "Put on your belt and your sandals."
He did so.
Then he said to him, "Put on your cloak and follow me."
So he followed him out,
    not realizing that what was happening through the angel
        was real;
    he thought he was seeing a vision.
They passed the first guard, then the second,
    and came to the iron gate leading out to the city,
    which opened for them by itself.
They emerged and made their way down an alley,
    and suddenly the angel left him.
Then Peter recovered his senses and said,
    "Now I know for certain
    that the Lord sent his angel
    and rescued me from the hand of Herod
    and from all that the Jewish people had been expecting."

The word of the Lord. **Thanks be to God.**

Responsorial Psalm (Psalm 34:2-3, 4-5, 6-7, 8-9)

R. **The angel of the Lord will rescue those who fear him.**

I will bless the LORD at all times;
    his praise shall be ever in my mouth.
Let my soul glory in the LORD;
    the lowly will hear me and be glad. R.

Glorify the LORD with me,
    let us together extol his name.
I sought the LORD, and he answered me
    and delivered me from all my fears. R.

Look to him that you may be radiant with joy,
    and your faces may not blush with shame.
When the poor one called out, the Lord heard,
    and from all his distress he saved him. R.

The angel of the LORD encamps
    around those who fear him, and delivers them.
Taste and see how good the LORD is;
    blessed the man who takes refuge in him. R.

Second Reading (2 Timothy 4:6-8, 17-18)

I, Paul, am already being poured out like a **libation**,
    and the **time of my departure** is at hand.
I have competed well; I have finished the **race**;
    I have kept the faith.
From now on the **crown** of righteousness awaits me,
    which the Lord, the just judge,
    will award to me on that day, and not only to me,
    but to all who have longed for his appearance.

The Lord stood by me and gave me strength,
    so that through me the proclamation might be completed
    and all the Gentiles might hear it.
And I was rescued from the lion's mouth.
The Lord will rescue me from every evil threat
    and will bring me safe to his heavenly Kingdom.
To him be glory forever and ever. Amen.

The word of the Lord. **Thanks be to God.**

Gospel (Matthew 16:13-19)

A reading from the holy Gospel according to Matthew.
Glory to you, O Lord.

When Jesus went into the region of Caesarea Philippi
    he asked his disciples,
    "Who do people say that the Son of Man is?"
They replied, "Some say John the Baptist, others Elijah,
    still others Jeremiah or one of the prophets."
He said to them, "But who do you say that I am?"
Simon Peter said in reply,
    "You are the Christ, the Son of the living God."
Jesus said to him in reply, "Blessed are you, Simon son of Jonah.
For flesh and blood has not revealed this to you, but my
heavenly Father.
And so I say to you, you are **Peter**,
    and upon this rock I will build my Church,
    and the gates of the netherworld shall not prevail against it.
I will give you the **keys** to the Kingdom of heaven.
Whatever you bind on earth shall be bound in heaven;
    and whatever you loose on earth shall be loosed in heaven."

The Gospel of the Lord. **Praise to you, Lord Jesus Christ.**

Key Words

Today's solemnity honors the martyrdoms in Rome of **Saint Peter and Saint Paul,** the two great apostles of the early Church. Both Peter and Paul were present at the Council of Jerusalem (Acts 15) where it was decided that believers did not need to convert to Judaism before being baptized as Christian. Peter would later become the first Bishop of Rome and Paul would become known as the Apostle to the Gentiles. They are thought to have been martyred at different times sometime between 64 and 68 AD.

The **Herod** mentioned in today's first reading was the grandson of Herod the Great who ruled at the time of Jesus' birth.

When Saint Paul writes to Timothy, he believes he is going to die soon – that the **time of his departure** is near. He has lived his life as a sacrifice given willingly to God – as a **libation,** or offering, poured out in service for the salvation of others.

Saint Paul uses the image of a **race** or sports contest to describe his work for the gospel – an image we can easily relate to. He has fought through to the end, and his prize, or medal, will be a **crown** – not of gold, silver, or bronze, but of righteousness.

When Simon shows both his understanding and his faith in Jesus as the Messiah, Jesus gives him a new name – **Peter** (from the Greek word *petra* for rock or stone). In many other languages, the name Peter is also related to rock or stone (such as *pierre* in French). Jesus is saying that Peter's faith will be the foundation for the Church's future.

Keys are a symbol of power. Whoever has the keys can enter and leave at will; they can also allow or deny entry to others. Jesus uses this symbol to show that Peter is the person with this power in the early Church.

July 6
14th Sunday in Ordinary Time

First Reading (Isaiah 66:10-14c)

Thus says the LORD:
Rejoice with **Jerusalem** and be glad because of her,
    all you who love her;
exult, exult with her,
    all you who were mourning over her!
Oh, that you may suck fully
    of the milk of her comfort,
that you may **nurse** with delight
    at her abundant breasts!
        For thus says the LORD:
Lo, I will spread prosperity over Jerusalem like a river,
    and the wealth of the nations like an overflowing torrent.
As nurslings, you shall be carried in her arms,
    and fondled in her lap;
as a mother comforts her child,
    so will I comfort you;
    in Jerusalem you shall find your comfort.

When you see this, your heart shall rejoice
    and your bodies flourish like the grass;
the LORD's power shall be known to his servants.

The word of the Lord. **Thanks be to God.**

Responsorial Psalm (Psalm 66:1-3, 4-5, 6-7, 16, 20)

R. **Let all the earth cry out to God with joy.**

Shout joyfully to God, all the earth,
    sing praise to the glory of his name;
    proclaim his glorious praise.
Say to God, "How **tremendous** are your deeds!" R.

"Let all on earth worship and sing praise to you,
    sing praise to your name!"
Come and see the works of God,
    his tremendous deeds among the children of Adam. R.

He has changed the sea into dry land;
  through the river they passed on foot;
  therefore let us rejoice in him.
He rules by his might forever. R.

Hear now, all you who fear God, while I declare
  what he has done for me.
Blessed be God who refused me not
  my prayer or his kindness! R.

Second Reading (Galatians 6:14-18)

Brothers and sisters: May I never boast except in the cross of our Lord Jesus Christ, through which the world has been crucified to me, and I to the world. For neither does circumcision mean anything, nor does uncircumcision, but only **a new creation**. Peace and mercy be to all who follow this rule and to the Israel of God.

From now on, let no one make troubles for me; for I bear the **marks of Jesus** on my body.

The grace of our Lord Jesus Christ be with your spirit, brothers and sisters. Amen.

The word of the Lord. **Thanks be to God.**

Gospel (Luke 10:1-12, 17-20)

For the shorter version, omit the indented parts in brackets.

A reading from the holy Gospel according to Luke.
Glory to you, O Lord.

At that time the Lord appointed seventy-two others whom he sent ahead of him in pairs to every town and place he intended to visit. He said to them, "The harvest is abundant but the laborers are few; so ask the **master of the harvest** to send out laborers for his harvest. Go on your way; behold, I am sending you like lambs among wolves. Carry no money bag, no sack, no sandals; and greet no one along the way. Into whatever house you enter, first say, 'Peace to this household.' If a peaceful person lives there, your peace will rest on him; but if not, it will return to you. Stay in the same house and eat and drink what is offered to you, for the laborer deserves his payment. Do not move about from one house to another. Whatever town you enter and they welcome you, eat what is set before you, cure the sick in it and say to them, 'The kingdom of God is at hand for you.'

[Whatever town you enter and they do not receive you, go out into the streets and say, 'The dust of your town that clings to our feet, even that we shake off against you.' Yet know this: the kingdom of God is at hand. I tell you, it will be more tolerable for Sodom on that day than for that town."

The seventy-two returned rejoicing, and said, "Lord, even the demons are subject to us because of your name." Jesus said, "I have observed Satan fall like lightning from the sky. Behold, I have given you the power to 'tread upon serpents' and scorpions and upon the full force of the enemy and nothing will harm you. Nevertheless, do not rejoice because the spirits are subject to you, but rejoice because your names are written in heaven."]

The Gospel of the Lord. **Praise to you, Lord Jesus Christ.**

Key Words

Not only was **Jerusalem** the name of the capital city of Israel, but it also became a poetic name for all the chosen people of God.

. . . .

When we hear the word **"nurse,"** we usually think of someone who cares for the sick. Nursing is also how a mother feeds her infant, using milk from her own body. The Prophet Isaiah is trying to explain how great are God's love and care for his people, and so he chooses an image of the strongest and fiercest love he can imagine — the love of a mother for her child.

. . . .

Tremendous deeds are acts that inspire wonder and surprise; they are majestic and thrilling.

. . . .

The Christians of Galatia began to get confused because some preachers were telling them that to be Christians, they first had to convert to Judaism and follow the entire Jewish law. Saint Paul wrote to the **Galatians** to reassure them and explain to them the importance of following Jesus' teachings.

. . . .

When Saint Paul speaks of **a new creation,** he is rejoicing in the new covenant. We are united with Jesus through baptism and faith, rather than through laws.

. . . .

The **marks of Jesus** that Saint Paul bears on his body are the physical signs of the sufferings he has endured — from flogging, illness, and imprisonment. He also calls them "brands" — permanent marks on the skin to show to whom he belongs. Paul proudly belongs to Christ.

. . . .

In today's gospel, the **master of the harvest** is God. We, the followers of Jesus, are workers in the fields, sowing the word of God to bring people back to God. The more workers there are, the more plentiful the harvest.

July 13

15th Sunday in Ordinary Time

First Reading (Deuteronomy 30:10-14)

Moses said to the people: "If only you would heed the voice of the LORD, your God, and keep his **commandments** and statutes that are written in this book of the law, when you return to the LORD, your God, with all your heart and all your soul.

"For this command that I enjoin on you today is not too mysterious and remote for you. It is not up in the sky, that you should say, 'Who will go up in the sky to get it for us and tell us of it, that we may carry it out?' Nor is it across the sea, that you should say, 'Who will cross the sea to get it for us and tell us of it, that we may carry it out?' No, it is something very near to you, already in your mouths and **in your hearts**; you have only to carry it out."

The word of the Lord. **Thanks be to God.**

An alternate psalm follows.

Responsorial Psalm (Psalm 69:14, 17, 30-31, 33-34, 36, 37)

R. **Turn to the Lord in your need, and you will live.**

I pray to you, O LORD,
    for the time of your favor, O God!
In your great kindness answer me
    with your constant help.
Answer me, O LORD, for bounteous is your kindness:
    in your great mercy turn toward me. R.

I am afflicted and in pain;
    let your saving help, O God, protect me.
I will praise the name of God in song,
    and I will glorify him with thanksgiving. R.

"See, you lowly ones, and be glad;
    you who seek God, may your hearts revive!
For the Lord hears the poor,
    and his own who are in bonds he spurns not." R.

For God will save Zion*
    and rebuild the cities of Judah.
The descendants of his servants shall inherit it,
    and those who love his name shall inhabit it. R.

Or

Responsorial Psalm (Psalm 19:8, 9, 10, 11)

R. **Your words, Lord, are Spirit and life.**

The law of the LORD is perfect,
   refreshing the soul;
the decree of the LORD is trustworthy,
   giving wisdom to the simple. R.

The precepts of the LORD are right,
   rejoicing the heart;
the command of the Lord is clear,
   enlightening the eye. R.

The fear of the LORD is pure,
   enduring forever;
the ordinances of the Lord are true,
   all of them just. R.

They are more precious than gold,
   than a heap of purest gold;
sweeter also than syrup
   or honey from the comb. R.

Second Reading (Colossians 1:15-20)

Christ Jesus is the image of the invisible God,
   the **firstborn** of all creation.
For in him were created all things in heaven and on earth,
   the visible and the invisible,
   whether **thrones or dominions or principalities or powers**;
   all things were created through him and for him.
He is before all things,
   and in him all things hold together.
He is the head of the body, the church.
He is the beginning, the firstborn from the dead,
   that in all things he himself might be preeminent.
For in him all the fullness was pleased to dwell,
   and through him to reconcile all things for him,
   making peace by the blood of his cross
   through him, whether those on earth or those in heaven.

The word of the Lord. **Thanks be to God.**

Gospel (Luke 10:25-37)

A reading from the holy Gospel according to Luke.
Glory to you, O Lord.

There was a **scholar of the law** who stood up to test him and said, "Teacher, what must I do to inherit eternal life?" Jesus said to him, "What is written in the law? How do you read it?" He said in reply, *"You shall love the Lord, your God, with all your heart, with all your being, with all your strength, and with all your mind, and your neighbor as yourself."* He replied to him, "You have answered correctly; do this and you will live."

But because he wished to justify himself, he said to Jesus, "And who is my neighbor?" Jesus replied, "A man fell victim to robbers as he went down from Jerusalem to Jericho. They stripped and beat him and went off leaving him half-dead. A priest happened to be going down that road, but when he saw him, he passed by on the opposite side. Likewise a **Levite** came to the place, and when he saw him, he passed by on the opposite side. But a **Samaritan** traveler who came upon him was moved with compassion at the sight. He approached the victim, poured oil and wine over his wounds and bandaged them. Then he lifted him up on his own animal, took him to an inn, and cared for him. The next day he took out two silver coins and gave them to the innkeeper with the instruction, 'Take care of him. If you spend more than what I have given you, I shall repay you on my way back.' Which of these three, in your opinion, was neighbor to the robbers' victim?" He answered, "The one who treated him with mercy." Jesus said to him, "Go and do likewise."

The Gospel of the Lord.
Praise to you, Lord Jesus Christ.

Key Words

Deuteronomy is a book in the Bible. In its pages are found the beliefs that there is one true God and that the people of God should be united. This name comes from the Greek word meaning "the second law" and refers to the second time that God gave the law to Moses. It was written 600 years before Christ.

A **commandment** is an order given by God that must be followed. The Ten Commandments are rules to live by that were given by God to the people through Moses. To obey the Ten Commandments is to live as faithful children of God.

God asks that you obey commandments gladly, that you hold them **in your heart,** as close as can be.

Jesus is the **firstborn** of all creation. Before he was born of the Virgin Mary — even before God created the world — he existed as the second person of the Trinity, the Son of God.

Thrones, dominions, principalities, or powers are names for the multitudes of angels in heaven in all their different categories. Angels are created by God who is greater and more powerful than all he has created.

A **scholar of the law** is an expert on laws who is trained to ask challenging questions. The lawyer in today's gospel is testing Jesus to see if he will make a mistake. But Jesus answers with truth and authority.

Levites were members of the tribe of Levi (one of the twelve tribes of Israel). They had the responsibility to carry and care for the Ark of the Covenant while the people wandered in the desert.

In Jesus' time the **Samaritans** and the Judeans did not get along well. They differed on many religious questions and were forbidden to speak to each other. People hearing the parable of the Good Samaritan would have been astounded that a Samaritan would stop to help someone who was traveling from Jerusalem, the holy city of the Jews.

July 20

16th Sunday in Ordinary Time

First Reading (Genesis 18:1-10a)

The LORD appeared to **Abraham** by the terebinth of Mamre, as he sat in the entrance of his tent, while the day was growing hot. Looking up, Abraham saw three men standing nearby. When he saw them, he ran from the entrance of the tent to greet them; and bowing to the ground, he said: "Sir, if I may ask you this favor, please do not go on past your servant. Let some water be brought, that you may bathe your feet, and then rest yourselves under the tree. Now that you have come this close to your servant, let me bring you a little food, that you may refresh yourselves; and afterward you may go on your way." The men replied, "Very well, do as you have said."

Abraham hastened into the tent and told Sarah, "Quick, three measures of fine flour! Knead it and make rolls." He ran to the herd, picked out a tender, choice steer, and gave it to a servant, who quickly prepared it. Then Abraham got some curds and milk, as well as the steer that had been prepared, and set these before the three men; and he waited on them under the tree while they ate.

They asked Abraham, "Where is your wife Sarah?" He replied, "There in the tent." One of them said, "I will surely return to you about this time next year, and Sarah will then have a son."

The word of the Lord. **Thanks be to God.**

Responsorial Psalm (Psalm 15:2-3, 3-4, 5)

R. **He who does justice will live in the presence of the Lord.**

One who walks blamelessly and does justice;
    who thinks the truth in his heart
    and slanders not with his tongue. R.

Who harms not his fellow man,
    nor takes up a reproach against his neighbor;
by whom the reprobate is despised,
    while he honors those who fear the LORD. R.

Who lends not his money at usury
  and accepts no bribe against the innocent.
One who does these things
  shall never be disturbed. R.

Second Reading (Colossians 1:24-28)

Brothers and sisters: Now I rejoice in my sufferings for your sake, and in my flesh I am filling up what is lacking in the **afflictions** of Christ on behalf of his body, which is the church, of which I am a minister in accordance with God's stewardship given to me to bring to completion for you the word of God, the mystery hidden from ages and from generations past. But now it has been manifested to his holy ones, to whom God chose to make known the riches of the glory of this **mystery** among the Gentiles; it is Christ in you, the hope for glory. It is he whom we proclaim, admonishing everyone and teaching everyone with all wisdom, that we may present everyone perfect in Christ.

The word of the Lord. **Thanks be to God.**

Gospel (Luke 10:38-42)

A reading from the holy Gospel according to Luke.
Glory to you, O Lord.

Jesus entered a village where a woman whose name was Martha welcomed him. She had a sister named Mary who sat beside the Lord at his feet listening to him speak. Martha, burdened with much serving, came to him and said, "Lord, do you not care that my sister has left me by myself to do the serving? Tell her to help me." The Lord said to her in reply, "Martha, Martha, you are anxious and worried about many things. There is need of only one thing. Mary has chosen **the better part** and it will not be taken from her."

The Gospel of the Lord. **Praise to you, Lord Jesus Christ.**

Abraham was the first man to have faith in the one true God. God rewarded Abraham's faithfulness by giving him a son, Isaac, from whom the people of Israel descended.

A **psalm** is a prayer that is sung. In the Bible, the book of Psalms has 150 prayers that reflect the way the people of Israel prayed. The psalms continue to teach us how to pray. In the Mass, after the first reading, a psalm is sung or said.

Saint Paul wrote a letter to the **Colossians,** members of a Christian community in the town of Colossae (in what is now Turkey). They were doubting their faith, but Paul's letter reminded them that Christ is above and before everything.

Saint Paul saw his own **afflictions** or suffering as part of the sufferings of Christ. Paul's hardships united him in a special way to Jesus, so that even though his life was hard, he found joy in his closeness to Jesus.

The **mystery** of God that Saint Paul mentions is God's plan for all humanity to be redeemed by his Son and live as children of God. This plan was revealed slowly by the prophets, until Jesus revealed it completely by his death and resurrection.

When Jesus says that Mary has chosen **the better part** over her sister Martha, he is letting us know that to be Jesus' friend — to listen to his word — is the most important thing to do. Martha would have done better to put her work aside for a while and honor Jesus with her presence and attention.

July 27

17th Sunday in Ordinary Time

First Reading (Genesis 18:20-32)

In those days, the LORD said: "The outcry against **Sodom and Gomorrah** is so great, and their sin so grave, that I must go down and see whether or not their actions fully correspond to the cry against them that comes to me. I mean to find out."

While Abraham's visitors walked on farther toward Sodom, the LORD remained standing before Abraham. Then Abraham drew nearer and said: "Will you sweep away the innocent with the guilty? Suppose there were fifty innocent people in the city; would you wipe out the place, rather than spare it for the sake of the fifty innocent people within it? Far be it from you to do such a thing, to make the innocent die with the guilty so that the innocent and the guilty would be treated alike! Should not the judge of all the world act with justice?" The LORD replied, "If I find fifty innocent people in the city of Sodom, I will spare the whole place for their sake." Abraham spoke up again: "See how I am presuming to speak to my LORD, though I am but **dust and ashes**! What if there are five less than fifty innocent people? Will you destroy the whole city because of those five?" He answered, "I will not destroy it, if I find forty-five there." But Abraham persisted, saying "What if only forty are found there?" He replied, "I will forbear doing it for the sake of the forty." Then Abraham said, "Let not my LORD grow impatient if I go on. What if only thirty are found there?" He replied, "I will forbear doing it if I can find but thirty there." Still Abraham went on, "Since I have thus dared to speak to my LORD, what if there are no more than twenty?" The LORD answered, "I will not destroy it, for the sake of the twenty." But he still persisted: "Please, let not my LORD grow angry if I speak up this last time. What if there are at least ten there?" He replied, "For the sake of those ten, I will not destroy it."

The word of the Lord. **Thanks be to God.**

Responsorial Psalm (Psalm 138:1-2, 2-3, 6-7, 7-8)

R. **Lord, on the day I called for help, you answered me.**

I will give thanks to you, O Lord, with all my heart,
    for you have heard the words of my mouth;
    in the presence of the angels I will sing your praise;
I will worship at your holy temple
    and give thanks to your name. R.

Because of your kindness and your truth;
    for you have made great above all things
    your name and your promise.
When I called you answered me;
    you built up strength within me. R.

The Lord is exalted, yet the lowly he sees,
    and the proud he knows from afar.
Though I walk amid distress, you preserve me;
    against the anger of my enemies you raise
        your hand. R.

Your right hand saves me.
    The Lord will complete what he has done for me;
your kindness, O Lord, endures forever;
    forsake not the work of your hands. R.

Second Reading (Colossians 2:12-14)

Brothers and sisters: You were buried with him in baptism, in which you were also raised with him through faith in the power of God, who raised him from the dead. And even when you were **dead in transgressions** and the uncircumcision of your flesh, he brought you to life along with him, having forgiven us all our transgressions; obliterating the bond against us, with its legal claims, which was opposed to us, he also removed it from our midst, nailing it to the cross.

The word of the Lord. **Thanks be to God.**

Gospel (Luke 11:1-13)

A reading from the holy Gospel according to Luke.
Glory to you, O Lord.

Jesus was **praying** in a certain place, and when he had finished, one of his disciples said to him, "Lord, teach us to pray just as John taught his disciples." He said to them, "When you pray, say:

> Father, **hallowed be your name**,
>> your kingdom come.
>> Give us each day our daily bread
>> and forgive us our sins
>> for we ourselves forgive everyone in debt to us,
>> and do not subject us to the final test."

And he said to them, "Suppose one of you has a friend to whom he goes at midnight and says, 'Friend, lend me three loaves of bread, for a friend of mine has arrived at my house from a journey and I have nothing to offer him,' and he says in reply from within, 'Do not bother me; the door has already been locked and my children and I are already in bed. I cannot get up to give you anything.' I tell you, if he does not get up to give the visitor the loaves because of their friendship, he will get up to give him whatever he needs because of his persistence.

"And I tell you, **ask and you will receive**; seek and you will find; knock and the door will be opened to you. For everyone who asks, receives; and the one who seeks, finds; and to the one who knocks, the door will be opened. What father among you would hand his son a snake when he asks for a fish? Or hand him a scorpion when he asks for an egg? If you then, who are wicked, know how to give good gifts to your children, how much more will the Father in heaven give the Holy Spirit to those who ask him?"

The Gospel of the Lord. **Praise to you, Lord Jesus Christ.**

Key Words

Genesis is the first book of the Bible. It tells many stories, including the stories of creation, Adam and Eve, the Flood, Abraham, and the people's faith in God. These stories help us understand that God loves us and wants us to love him too.

The two cities of **Sodom and Gomorrah** had disappeared by Jesus' time, but their story in the book of Genesis was well known. They were mentioned as symbols of evil; there were no worse cities than these two.

When Abraham calls himself **dust and ashes,** he expresses how small he feels before God. It is a way of saying that he is worth very little — too worthless to make a petition to God. The dust also reminds us that God created human beings from dust (in the Book of Genesis).

To be **dead in transgressions** is to be burdened by the weight of our sins. When we are united to Jesus through baptism, and ask for God's forgiveness for our sins, we find new life in Jesus.

Jesus was frequently found **praying,** especially during the most important moments of his life. It is very important for all of us to learn to quiet our hearts in order to speak and listen to God.

In the Lord's Prayer, when we say "**hallowed be** thy **name,**" we are declaring that God's name should be made holy or hallowed. It is a way of saying, "Blessed be you" — your holiness and grandeur will be known everywhere.

Jesus said, **"ask and you will receive."** This teaches us to have every confidence that God listens to us and will always give us what we most need in order to live as God's children.

August 3

18th Sunday in Ordinary Time

First Reading (Ecclesiastes 1:2; 2:21-23)

Vanity of vanities, says Qoheleth,
  vanity of vanities! All things are vanity!

Here is one who has labored with wisdom and knowledge and skill, and yet to another who has not labored over it, he must leave property. This also is vanity and a great misfortune. For what profit comes to man from all the toil and anxiety of heart with which he has labored under the sun? All his days sorrow and grief are his occupation; even at night his mind is not at rest. This also is vanity.

The word of the Lord. **Thanks be to God.**

Responsorial Psalm (Psalm 90:3-4, 5-6, 12-13, 14 and 17)

R. **If today you hear his voice, harden not your hearts.**

You turn man back to dust,
  saying, "Return, O children of men."
For a thousand years in your sight
  are as yesterday, now that it is past,
  or as a watch of the night. R.

You make an end of them in their sleep;
  the next morning they are like the changing grass,
Which at dawn springs up anew,
  but by evening wilts and fades. R.

Teach us to number our days aright,
  that we may gain wisdom of heart.
Return, O Lord! How long?
  Have pity on your servants! R.

Fill us at daybreak with your kindness,
  that we may shout for joy and gladness all our days.
And may the gracious care of the Lord our God be ours;
  prosper the work of our hands for us!
  Prosper the work of our hands! R.

Second Reading (Colossians 3:1-5, 9-11)

Brothers and sisters: If you were raised with Christ, seek **what is above**, where Christ is seated at the right hand of God. Think of what is above, not of what is on earth. For you have died, and your life is hidden with Christ in God. When Christ your life appears, then you too will **appear with him in glory**.

Put to death, then, the parts of you that are earthly: immorality, impurity, passion, evil desire, and the **greed** that is idolatry. Stop lying to one another, since you have taken off the old self with its practices and have put on the new self, which is being renewed, for knowledge, in the image of its creator. Here there is not Greek and Jew, circumcision and uncircumcision, barbarian, Scythian, slave, free; but Christ is all and in all.

The word of the Lord. **Thanks be to God.**

Gospel (Luke 12:13-21)

A reading from the holy Gospel according to Luke.
Glory to you, O Lord.

Someone in the crowd said to Jesus, "Teacher, tell my brother to share the inheritance with me." He replied to him, "Friend, who appointed me as your judge and arbitrator?" Then he said to the crowd, "Take care to guard against all greed, for though one may be rich, one's life does not consist of possessions."

Then he told them a parable. "There was a rich man whose land produced a bountiful harvest. He asked himself, 'What shall I do, for I do not have space to store my harvest?' And he said, 'This is what I shall do: I shall tear down my barns and build larger ones. There I shall store all my grain and other goods and I shall say to myself, "Now as for you, you have so many good things stored up for many years, rest, eat, drink, be merry!" ' But God said to him, 'You fool, this night your life will be demanded of you; and the things you have prepared, to whom will they belong?' Thus will it be for all who store up treasure for themselves but are not **rich in what matters to God**."

The Gospel of the Lord. **Praise to you, Lord Jesus Christ.**

Key Words

Ecclesiastes is a book in the Old Testament written 300 years before Christ. Its message is not to worry about every little thing, but to take pleasure in God's gifts and to keep God's commandments.

When Saint Paul mentions **what is above,** he is referring to all that helps us live as children of God, following the teachings of Jesus. The things that are of earth are those things that fill us with worry or lead us away from Jesus.

As Christians we are all called to **appear with him** (Jesus) **in glory** — to live in such a way that it is clear to others that we are close to Jesus. When Jesus comes again, all who have died will be gathered to him in glory.

Greed is an urge in our hearts for more things, more money, more clothes, more toys... even though we don't need them. When we are ruled by greed, we forget that there are people more in need than ourselves.

We are **rich in what matters to God** when we reject greed and live as brothers and sisters — helping those who are in need, the sick, the poor, the lonely. Our wealth is measured not by our worldly possessions but by how we live.

August 10
19th Sunday in Ordinary Time

First Reading (Wisdom 18:6-9)

The night of the passover was known beforehand
    to our fathers,
    that, with sure knowledge of the oaths in which
        they put their faith,
    they might have courage.
Your people awaited the salvation of the just
    and the destruction of their foes.
For when you punished our adversaries,
    in this you glorified us whom you had summoned.
For in secret the holy children of the good
        were offering sacrifice
    and putting into effect with one accord
        the divine institution.

The word of the Lord. **Thanks be to God.**

Responsorial Psalm (Psalm 33:1, 12, 18-19, 20-22)

R̶. **Blessed the people the Lord has chosen to be his own.**

Exult, you just, in the LORD;
    praise from the upright is fitting.
Blessed the nation whose God is the LORD,
    the people he has chosen for his own inheritance. R̶.

See, the eyes of the LORD are upon those who fear him,
    upon those who hope for his kindness,
to deliver them from death
    and preserve them in spite of famine. R̶.

Our soul waits for the LORD,
    who is our help and our shield.
May your kindness, O LORD, be upon us
    who have put our hope in you. R̶.

Second Reading (Hebrews 11:1-2, 8-19)

The shorter version ends at the asterisks.

Brothers and sisters: Faith is the realization of what is hoped for and evidence of things not seen. Because of it the ancients were well attested.

By faith Abraham obeyed when he was called to go out to a place that he was to receive as an inheritance; he went out, not knowing where he was to go. By faith he sojourned in the promised land as in a foreign country, dwelling in tents with **Isaac** and **Jacob**, heirs of the same promise; for he was looking forward to the city with foundations, whose architect and maker is God. By faith he received power to generate, even though he was past the normal age—and Sarah herself was sterile—for he thought that the one who had made the promise was trustworthy. So it was that there came forth from one man, himself as good as dead, descendants as numerous as the stars in the sky and as countless as the sands on the seashore.

* * *

All these died in faith. They did not receive what had been promised but saw it and greeted it from afar and acknowledged themselves to be strangers and aliens on earth, for those who speak thus show that they are seeking a homeland. If they had been thinking of the land from which they had come, they would have had opportunity to return. But now they desire a better homeland, a heavenly one. Therefore, God is not ashamed to be called their God, for he has prepared a city for them.

By faith Abraham, when put to the test, offered up Isaac, and he who had received the promises was ready to offer his only son, of whom it was said, "Through Isaac descendants shall bear your name." He reasoned that God was able to raise even from the dead, and he received Isaac back as a symbol.

The word of the Lord. **Thanks be to God.**

Gospel (Luke 12:32-48)

For the shorter version, omit the indented parts in brackets.

A reading from the holy Gospel according to Luke.
Glory to you, O Lord.

Jesus said to his disciples:

["Do not be afraid any longer, little flock, for your Father is pleased to give you the kingdom. Sell your belongings and give alms. Provide money bags for yourselves that do not wear out, an inexhaustible treasure in heaven that no thief can reach nor moth destroy. For where your treasure is, there also will your heart be.]

"Gird your loins and light your lamps and be like servants who await their master's return from a **wedding**, ready to open immediately when he comes and knocks. Blessed are those servants whom the master finds vigilant on his arrival. Amen, I say to you, he will gird himself, have them recline at table, and proceed to wait on them. And should he come in the second or third watch and find them prepared in this way, blessed are those servants. Be sure of this: if the master of the house had known the hour when the thief was coming, he would not have let his house be broken into. You also must be prepared, for at an hour you do not expect, the **Son of Man** will come."

[Then Peter said, "Lord, is this parable meant for us or for everyone?" And the Lord replied, "Who, then, is the faithful and prudent steward whom the master will put in charge of his servants to distribute the food allowance at the proper time? Blessed is that servant whom his master on arrival finds doing so. Truly, I say to you, the master will put the servant in charge of all his property. But if that servant says to himself, 'My master is delayed in coming,' and begins to beat the menservants and the maidservants, to eat and drink and get drunk, then that servant's master will come on an unexpected day and at an unknown hour and will punish the servant severely and assign him a place with the unfaithful. That servant who knew his master's will but did not make preparations nor act in accord with his will shall be beaten severely; and the servant who was ignorant of his master's will but acted in a way deserving of a severe beating shall be beaten only lightly. Much will be required of the person entrusted with much, and still more will be demanded of the person entrusted with more."]

The Gospel of the Lord. **Praise to you, Lord Jesus Christ.**

Key Words

The book of **Wisdom** is part of the Old Testament written shortly before Jesus was born. It teaches that the truly wise person lives a faithful life and strives for justice.

The Letter to the **Hebrews** is found in the New Testament. Its author is unknown. More than a letter, it appears to be a very solemn sermon. It encourages us to remember that Jesus Christ is our merciful priest who offered his life as a sacrifice on our behalf.

Isaac, the son of Abraham and Sarah, inherited the promise made to Abraham that he would father a great family. This family would become the chosen people of God. **Jacob** was the son of Isaac and Rebecca; he cleverly won this promised inheritance from his twin brother, Esau. Jacob had twelve sons who founded the twelve tribes of Israel.

A **wedding** banquet is a joyous reception held after two people get married. The Bible often refers to the arrival of the reign of God as such a feast where all people will be welcome. It will be a time of great joy and celebration.

In the gospels, Jesus calls himself the **Son of Man.** Jesus uses this title to show he is a human being, and tells his disciples that although he will suffer greatly, his suffering will not overcome him.

August 15
The Assumption of the Blessed Virgin Mary

Mass During the Day

First Reading (Revelation 11:19a; 12:1-6a, 10ab)

God's temple in heaven was opened, and the ark of his covenant could be seen in the temple.

A great sign appeared in the sky, a **woman clothed with the sun**, with the moon under her feet, and on her head a crown of twelve stars. She was with child and wailed aloud in pain as she labored to give birth. Then another sign appeared in the sky; it was a huge red dragon, with seven heads and ten horns, and on its heads were seven diadems. Its tail swept away a third of the stars in the sky and hurled them down to the earth. Then the dragon stood before the woman about to give birth, to devour her child when she gave birth. She gave birth to a son, a male child, destined to rule all the nations with an iron rod. Her child was caught up to God and his throne. The woman herself fled into the desert where she had a place prepared by God.

Then I heard a loud voice in heaven say:
"Now have salvation and power come,
and the Kingdom of our God
and the authority of his Anointed One."

The word of the Lord. **Thanks be to God.**

Responsorial Psalm (Psalm 45:10, 11, 12, 16)

℟. **The queen stands at your right hand, arrayed in gold.**

The queen takes her place at your right hand
in gold of Ophir. ℟.

Hear, O daughter, and see; turn your ear,
forget your people and your father's house. ℟.

So shall the king desire your beauty;
for he is your lord. ℟.

They are borne in with gladness and joy;
they enter the palace of the king. ℟.

Second Reading (1 Corinthians 15:20-27)

Brothers and sisters: Christ has been raised from the dead, the **firstfruits** of those who have fallen asleep. For since death came through man, the resurrection of the dead came also through man. For just as in Adam all die, so too in Christ shall all be brought to life, but each one in proper order: Christ the firstfruits; then, at his coming, those who belong to Christ; then comes the end, when he hands over the Kingdom to his God and Father, when he has destroyed every sovereignty and every authority and power. For he must reign until he has put all his enemies under his feet. The last enemy to be destroyed is death, for "he subjected everything under his feet."

The word of the Lord. **Thanks be to God.**

Gospel (Luke 1:39-56)

A reading from the holy Gospel according to Luke.
Glory to you, O Lord.

Mary set out and traveled to the hill country in haste to a town of Judah, where she entered the house of Zechariah* and greeted Elizabeth. When Elizabeth heard Mary's greeting, the infant leaped in her womb, and Elizabeth, filled with the Holy Spirit, cried out in a loud voice and said, "Blessed are you among women, and blessed is the fruit of your womb. And how does this happen to me, that the mother of my Lord should come to me? For at the moment the sound of your greeting reached my ears, the infant in my womb leaped for joy. Blessed are you who believed that what was spoken to you by the Lord would be fulfilled."

And Mary said:
    "**My soul proclaims the greatness of the Lord**;
        my spirit rejoices in God my Savior
        for he has looked with favor on his lowly servant.
    From this day all generations will call me blessed:
        the Almighty has done great things for me
        and holy is his Name.
        He has mercy on those who fear him
        in every generation.
    He has shown the strength of his arm,
        and has scattered the proud in their conceit.

He has cast down the mighty from their thrones,
and has lifted up the lowly.
He has filled the hungry with good things,
and the rich he has sent away empty.
He has come to the help of his servant Israel
for he has remembered his promise of mercy,
the promise he made to our fathers,
to Abraham and his children forever."

Mary remained with her about three months and then returned to her home.

The Gospel of the Lord. **Praise to you, Lord Jesus Christ.**

Key Words

Today's first reading portrays the conflict between Jesus Christ and the power of evil (Satan) through the story of a huge red dragon and a **woman clothed with the sun**. The woman could represent God's people—either as Israel giving birth to the Messiah or as the Church being persecuted by Satan—or Mary, enduring the pain of birth for a son "destined to rule all the nations."

The **firstfruits** were the first crops collected at harvest time. These were offered to God. Saint Paul tells us that Jesus is the firstfruits of salvation, the first to die and rise again. Jesus Christ is our guarantee that death is not the end but rather a transition to new life.

Mary's prayer that begins, **"My soul proclaims the greatness of the Lord**…" is known as the Magnificat (the first word in the Latin version of this prayer). It is an ancient prayer of triumph through humility that leads us to Christ. When we make it our prayer, too, it calls us to recognize God's saving work in our lives. It teaches us the true meaning of humility and invites us to submit our will to God. Mary recognized that God's design for the world will reverse the way humans have set things up.

August 17

20th Sunday in Ordinary Time

First Reading (Jeremiah 38:4-6, 8-10)

In those days, the princes said to the king: "Jeremiah ought to be put to death; he is demoralizing the soldiers who are left in this city, and all the people, by speaking such things to them; he is not interested in the welfare of our people, but in their ruin." King **Zedekiah** answered: "He is in your power"; for the king could do nothing with them. And so they took Jeremiah and threw him into the **cistern** of Prince Malchiah, which was in the quarters of the guard, letting him down with ropes. There was no water in the cistern, only mud, and Jeremiah sank into the mud.

Ebed-melech, a court official, went there from the palace and said to him: "My lord king, these men have been at fault in all they have done to the prophet Jeremiah, casting him into the cistern. He will die of famine on the spot, for there is no more food in the city." Then the king ordered Ebed-melech the Cushite to take three men along with him, and draw the prophet Jeremiah out of the cistern before he should die.

The word of the Lord. **Thanks be to God.**

Responsorial Psalm (Psalm 40:2, 3, 4, 18)

R. **Lord, come to my aid!**

I have waited, waited for the LORD,
   and he stooped toward me. R.

The LORD heard my cry.
He drew me out of the pit of destruction,
   out of the mud of the **swamp**;
he set my feet upon a crag;
   he made firm my steps. R.

And he put a new song into my mouth,
   a hymn to our God.
Many shall look on in awe
   and trust in the LORD. R.

> Though I am afflicted and poor,
>   yet the LORD thinks of me.
> You are my help and my deliverer;
>   O my God, hold not back! R.

Second Reading (Hebrews 12:1-4)

Brothers and sisters: Since we are surrounded by so great a **cloud of witnesses**, let us rid ourselves of every burden and sin that clings to us and persevere in running the race that lies before us while keeping our eyes fixed on Jesus, the leader and **perfecter** of faith. For the sake of the joy that lay before him he endured the cross, despising its shame, and has taken his seat at the right of the throne of God. Consider how he endured such opposition from sinners, in order that you may not grow weary and lose heart. In your struggle against sin you have not yet resisted to the point of shedding blood.

The word of the Lord. **Thanks be to God.**

Gospel (Luke 12:49-53)

A reading from the holy Gospel according to Luke.
Glory to you, O Lord.

Jesus said to his disciples: "I have come to set the earth on fire, and how I wish it were already blazing! There is a baptism with which I must be baptized, and how great is my anguish until it is accomplished! Do you think that I have come to **establish peace** on the earth? No, I tell you, but rather division. From now on a household of five will be divided, three against two and two against three; a father will be divided against his son and a son against his father, a mother against her daughter and a daughter against her mother, a mother-in-law against her daughter-in-law and a daughter-in-law against her mother-in-law."

The Gospel of the Lord. **Praise to you, Lord Jesus Christ.**

Key Words

Zedekiah was king of Israel at the time of the prophet Jeremiah. Jeremiah was the king's counselor, but the king did not treat Jeremiah well.

. . . .

A **cistern** is a deep structure, like a well, where water is collected for future use. Cisterns are commonly found in areas with little rainfall. Because they are so deep, they are dangerous, wet or dry.

. . . .

A **swamp** is an impassable muddy bog. This psalm echoes the story of Jeremiah that we have just heard, where Jeremiah is thrown into a cistern with a deep, muddy bottom.

. . . .

The **cloud of witnesses** that surrounds us is made up of the saints and good Christians who came before us and showed us by their example how to live our faith. We are strengthened and supported by this great communion of saints.

Although many holy priests and prophets came before Jesus, he was the **perfecter** of our faith, because he explained the writings and fulfilled the prophecies through his life, death, and resurrection.

. . . .

To **establish peace** is to bring tranquillity and the absence of strife to a situation. Why would Jesus say he has not come to bring peace? Jesus is telling us that we must make radical changes to our lives in order to follow him and then find peace. Following the path of Jesus leads through death to new life.

August 24
21st Sunday in Ordinary Time

First Reading (Isaiah 66:18-21)

Thus says the LORD: I know their works and their thoughts, and I come to gather **nations** of every language; they shall come and see my glory. I will set a sign among them; from them I will send fugitives to the nations: to Tarshish, Put and Lud, Mosoch, Tubal and Javan, to the distant coastlands that have never heard of my fame, or seen my glory; and they shall proclaim my **glory** among the nations. They shall bring all your brothers and sisters from all the nations as an offering to the LORD, on horses and in chariots, in carts, upon mules and dromedaries, to **Jerusalem**, my holy mountain, says the LORD, just as the Israelites bring their offering to the house of the LORD in clean vessels. Some of these I will take as priests and Levites, says the LORD.

The word of the Lord. **Thanks be to God.**

Responsorial Psalm (Psalm 117:1, 2)

R. **Go out to all the world and tell the Good News.**
Or **Alleluia.**

Praise the LORD, all you nations;
    glorify him, all you peoples! R.

For steadfast is his kindness toward us,
    and the fidelity of the LORD endures forever. R.

Second Reading (Hebrews 12:5-7, 11-13)

Brothers and sisters, You have forgotten the exhortation addressed to you as children: "My son, do not disdain the **discipline** of the Lord or lose heart when reproved by him; for whom the Lord loves, he disciplines; he scourges every son he acknowledges." Endure your trials as "discipline"; God treats you as sons. For what "son" is there whom his father does not discipline? At the time, all discipline seems a cause not for joy but for pain, yet later it brings the peaceful fruit of righteousness to those who are trained by it.

So strengthen your drooping hands and your weak knees. Make straight paths for your feet, that what is lame may not be disjointed but healed.

The word of the Lord. **Thanks be to God.**

Gospel (Luke 13:22-30)

A reading from the holy Gospel according to Luke.
Glory to you, O Lord.

Jesus passed through towns and villages, teaching as he went and making his way to Jerusalem. Someone asked him, "Lord, will only a few people be saved?" He answered them, "Strive to enter through the **narrow gate**, for many, I tell you, will attempt to enter but will not be strong enough. After the master of the house has arisen and locked the door, then will you stand outside knocking and saying, 'Lord, open the door for us.' He will say to you in reply, 'I do not know where you are from.' And you will say, 'We ate and drank in your company and you taught in our streets.' Then he will say to you, 'I do not know where you are from. Depart from me, all you evildoers!' And there will be wailing and grinding of teeth when you see Abraham, Isaac, and Jacob and all the prophets in the **kingdom** of God and you yourselves cast out. And people will come from the east and the west and from the north and the south and will recline at table in the kingdom of God. For behold, some are last who will be first, and some are first who will be last."

The Gospel of the Lord. **Praise to you, Lord Jesus Christ.**

Key Words

When Isaiah mentions gathering all **nations,** he is describing people coming from all the ends of the Earth. Tarshish is in Spain; Put and Lud are in Africa; Tubal is near Russia; and Javan is in Greece. Everyone will meet in Jerusalem.

To see the **glory** of God means to recognize God's importance, power, and authority. It is to accept the true God.

The moment when all the people in the world arrive in **Jerusalem,** the city of peace, is the moment when all humanity will be united in faith to their Creator, who led the people of Israel out of slavery in Egypt.

The letter to the Hebrews teaches us to see **discipline** or correction from God as an opportunity to grow. God can use even our sufferings to help us live better lives and grow in love.

To enter an area by a **narrow gate** is not an easy thing to do: it takes some effort. Jesus uses this image in order to tell us to be persistent in doing good and loving our neighbor. This way, our friendship will grow with Jesus and we will enter the kingdom of heaven.

When Jesus speaks of the **kingdom** of God, he means the end of time when God's reign will be complete and when all people will live in unity and peace.

August 31

22nd Sunday in Ordinary Time

First Reading (Sirach 3:17-18, 20, 28-29)

My child, conduct your affairs with **humility**,
and you will be loved more than a giver of gifts.
Humble yourself the more, the greater you are,
    and you will find favor with God.
What is too sublime for you, seek not,
    into things beyond your strength search not.
The mind of a sage appreciates proverbs,
    and an attentive ear is the joy of the wise.
Water quenches a flaming fire,
    and alms atone for sins.

The word of the Lord. **Thanks be to God.**

Responsorial Psalm (Psalm 68:4-5, 6-7, 10-11)

℟. **God, in your goodness, you have made a home for the poor.**

The just rejoice and exult before God;
    they are glad and rejoice.
Sing to God, chant praise to his name;
    whose name is the LORD. ℟.

The father of orphans and the defender of widows
    is God in his holy dwelling.
God gives a home to the forsaken;
    he leads forth prisoners to prosperity. ℟.

A bountiful rain you showered down, O God,
      upon your inheritance;
    you restored the land when it languished;
your flock settled in it;
      in your goodness, O God, you provided it for
        the needy. ℟.

Second Reading (Hebrews 12:18-19, 22-24a)

Brothers and sisters: You have not approached that which could be touched and a blazing fire and gloomy darkness and storm and a trumpet blast and a voice speaking words such that those who heard begged that no message be further addressed to them. No, you have approached **Mount Zion** and the city of the living God, **the heavenly Jerusalem**, and countless angels in festal gathering, and the assembly of the firstborn enrolled in heaven, and God the judge of all, and the spirits of the just made perfect, and Jesus, the mediator of a new covenant, and the sprinkled blood that speaks more eloquently than that of Abel.

The word of the Lord. **Thanks be to God.**

Gospel (Luke 14:1, 7-14)

A reading from the holy Gospel according to Luke.
Glory to you, O Lord.

On a sabbath Jesus went to dine at the home of one of the leading **Pharisees**, and the people there were observing him carefully.

He told a parable to those who had been invited, noticing how they were choosing the places of honor at the table. "When you are invited by someone to a wedding banquet, do not recline at table in the place of honor. A more distinguished guest than you may have been invited by him, and the host who invited both of you may approach you and say, 'Give your place to this man,' and then you would proceed with embarrassment to take the lowest place. Rather, when you are invited, go and take the lowest place so that when the host comes to you he may say, 'My friend, move up to a higher position.' Then you will enjoy the esteem of your companions at the table. For every one who exalts himself will be humbled, but the one who humbles himself will be exalted." Then he said to the host who invited him, "When you hold a lunch or a dinner, do not invite your friends or your brothers or your relatives or your wealthy neighbors, in case they may invite you back and you have repayment. Rather, when you hold a banquet, **invite the poor**, the crippled, the lame, the blind; blessed indeed will you be because of their inability to repay you. For you will be repaid at the resurrection of the righteous."

The Gospel of the Lord. **Praise to you, Lord Jesus Christ.**

Key Words

The book of **Sirach** was written 200 years before Jesus was born. It deals with many topics, but especially with the nature of true wisdom: respect for God and obedience to God's plans for us.

When we have true **humility,** we learn to value ourselves as children of God. We do not feel overly important, but we also do not undervalue the wonderful qualities that God has given to each of us.

Mount Zion was another name for the city of Jerusalem, which was very close to this rocky peak. Sometimes the great Temple in Jerusalem was also referred to by this name.

One way to speak of the place where, at the end of time, God will meet all those who have died in Christ is to refer to **the heavenly Jerusalem.**

The **Pharisees** were Jews who belonged to a very strict sect and followed all the religious rules but sometimes forgot to live with love. They were not well liked among the common people.

According to Jesus, the most important thing is to learn how to be generous, for real generosity expects nothing in return. He challenges his host, the Pharisee who invited him to dinner, next time to **invite the poor** who have no hope of repaying the favor. The invitation is then a pure gift, given in generous love.

September 7

23rd Sunday in Ordinary Time

First Reading (Wisdom 9:13-18b)

Who can know God's **counsel**,
    or who can conceive what the LORD intends?
For the deliberations of mortals are timid,
    and unsure are our plans.
For the corruptible body burdens the soul
    and the earthen shelter weighs down the mind
        that has many concerns.
And scarce do we guess the things on earth,
    and what is within our grasp we find with difficulty;
    but when things are in heaven, who can search them out?
Or who ever knew your counsel, except you had given **wisdom**
    and sent your holy spirit from on high?
And thus were the paths of those on earth made straight.

The word of the Lord. **Thanks be to God.**

Responsorial Psalm (Psalm 90:3-4, 5-6, 12-13, 14 and 17)

R. **In every age, O Lord, you have been our refuge.**

You turn man back to dust,
    saying, "Return, O children of men."
For a thousand years in your sight
    are as yesterday, now that it is past,
    or as a watch of the night. R.

You make an end of them in their sleep;
    the next morning they are like the changing grass,
Which at dawn springs up anew,
    but by evening wilts and fades. R.

Teach us to number our days aright,
    that we may gain wisdom of heart.
Return, O LORD! How long?
    Have pity on your servants! R.

Fill us at daybreak with your kindness,
    that we may shout for joy and gladness all our days.
And may the gracious care of the LORD our God be ours;
    prosper the work of our hands for us!
    Prosper the work of our hands! R.

Second Reading (Philemon 9-10, 12-17)

I, Paul, an old man, and now also a prisoner for Christ Jesus, urge you on behalf of my child Onesimus, **whose father I have become** in my imprisonment; I am sending him, that is, my own heart, back to you. I should have liked to retain him for myself, so that he might serve me on your behalf in my imprisonment for the gospel, but I did not want to do anything without your consent, so that the good you do might not be forced but voluntary. Perhaps this is why he was away from you for a while, that you might have him back forever, no longer as a slave but more than a slave, a brother, beloved especially to me, but even more so to you, as a man and in the Lord. So if you regard me as a partner, welcome him as you would me.

The word of the Lord. **Thanks be to God.**

Gospel (Luke 14:25-33)

A reading from the holy Gospel according to Luke.
Glory to you, O Lord.

Great crowds were traveling with Jesus, and he turned and addressed them, "If anyone **comes to me** without hating his father and mother, wife and children, brothers and sisters, and even his own life, he cannot be my disciple. Whoever does not carry his own cross and come after me **cannot be my disciple.** Which of you wishing to construct a tower does not first sit down and calculate the cost to see if there is enough for its completion? Otherwise, after laying the foundation and finding himself unable to finish the work the onlookers should laugh at him and say, 'This one began to build but did not have the resources to finish.' Or what king marching into battle would not first sit down and decide whether with ten thousand troops he can successfully oppose another king advancing upon him with twenty thousand troops? But if not, while he is still far away, he will send a delegation to ask for peace terms. In the same way, anyone of you who does not renounce all his possessions cannot be my disciple."

The Gospel of the Lord. **Praise to you, Lord Jesus Christ.**

Key Words

The **counsel** or wisdom of God is God's plan for us, for all people and all creation. We cannot know the mind of God, but we can learn from the wisdom of the prophets and the Church.

. . . .

Wisdom is not something that comes from studying hard. Wisdom comes from prayer and lived experience; it is a gift of the Holy Spirit that helps us to make good decisions.

. . . .

The letter written by Saint Paul to **Philemon** is a short but beautiful letter. It teaches that, for Christians, all men and women are equal: there should be no difference between Jews and Gentiles, or between slaves and free people, because we are all brothers and sisters as children of God.

Saint Paul wrote to Philemon about having baptized Onesimus in jail, **"whose father I have become"** for Christ. Through baptism, Paul gave his friend life in the Spirit of God and, in this sense, became his "spiritual father."

. . . .

To follow Jesus means to decide to live as he lived, loving God above all else. Someone **"comes to me,"** God says, if they follow Jesus and live justly, treating all people as their brothers and sisters.

. . . .

A person **"cannot be my disciple,"** Jesus says, if they are unable to give up everything else, even the best things in life. We have to be ready to leave even our most cherished possessions. This is a hard teaching; Jesus calls it our "cross."

September 14

Exaltation of the Holy Cross

First Reading (Numbers 21:4b-9)

With their patience worn out by the journey,
  the people complained against God and Moses,
  "Why have you brought us up from Egypt to die in this desert,
  where there is no food or water?
We are disgusted with this wretched food!"
In punishment the Lord sent among the people saraph serpents,
  which bit the people so that many of them died.
Then the people came to Moses and said,
  "We have sinned in complaining against the LORD and you.
Pray the LORD to take the serpents from us."
So Moses prayed for the people, and the LORD said to Moses,
  "Make a saraph and mount it on a pole,
  and if any who have been bitten look at it, they will live."
Moses accordingly made a bronze **serpent** and mounted it on a
pole, and whenever anyone who had been bitten by a serpent
looked at the bronze serpent, he lived.

The word of the Lord. **Thanks be to God.**

Responsorial Psalm (Psalm 78:1bc-2, 34-35, 36-37, 38)

R. **Do not forget the works of the Lord!**

Hearken, my people, to my teaching;
    incline your ears to the words of my mouth.
I will open my mouth in a parable,
    I will utter mysteries from of old. R.

While he slew them they sought him
    and inquired after God again,
Remembering that God was their rock
    and the Most High God, their redeemer. R.

But they flattered him with their mouths
    and lied to him with their tongues,
Though their hearts were not steadfast toward him,
    nor were they faithful to his covenant. R.

But he, being merciful, forgave their sin
    and destroyed them not;
Often he turned back his anger
    and let none of his wrath be roused. R.

Second Reading (Philippians 2:6-11)

Brothers and sisters:
  Christ Jesus, though he was in the form of God,
    did not regard equality with God something to be grasped.
  Rather, he emptied himself,
  taking the form of a slave,
  coming in human likeness;
  and found human in appearance,
  he humbled himself,
  becoming obedient to death,
      even death on a cross.
Because of this, God greatly exalted him
  and bestowed on him the name
  that is above every name,
  that at the name of Jesus
  every knee should bend,
  of those in heaven and on earth and under the earth,
  and every tongue confess that
  Jesus **Christ** is Lord,
  to the glory of God the Father.

The word of the Lord. **Thanks be to God.**

Gospel (John 3:13-17)

Jesus said to Nicodemus:
"No one has gone up to heaven
except the one who has come down from heaven, the Son ofMan.
And just as Moses lifted up the serpent in the desert,
  so must the Son of Man be lifted up,
  so that everyone who believes in him may have eternal life."

For God so loved the world that he gave his only Son,
  so that everyone who believes in him might not perish
  but might have eternal life.
For God did not send his Son into the world to condemn the world,
  but that the world might be saved through him.

The Gospel of the Lord. **Praise to you, Lord Jesus Christ.**

Key Words

Today we celebrate the feast of the **Exaltation** of the Cross, a feast which originated in 4th-century Jerusalem. On September 14, 320 AD, the true cross (as it was believed to be) was raised or exalted when two churches built by the Emperor Constantine were consecrated. On Good Friday, the cross is raised, or exalted, so that we can venerate it (show reverence).

This reading from the Book of Numbers begins: **With their patience worn out**. These are the days, or years, when the people of Israel were wandering in the desert after Moses freed them from slavery in Egypt. They had not yet reached the Promised Land, and were often weary and impatient.

When the Israelites wandered through the desert, they encountered poisonous snakes. God told Moses to make a bronze **serpent** and lift it up on a pole, like a flag. Anyone who was bitten by a snake and looked at the bronze serpent was healed. In today's gospel, Jesus tells Nicodemus that when he, Jesus, is lifted up on the cross and then raised from the dead, he will bring eternal life to all people who believe in him.

The name **Christ Jesus** or **Jesus Christ** brings together two words: Jesus, which means 'God saves,' the name that his parents gave him; and **Christ**, which means 'anointed,' the person chosen by God to be a true prophet, priest, and king.

September 21

25th Sunday in Ordinary Time

First Reading (Amos 8:4-7)

Hear this, you who trample upon the needy
and destroy the poor of the land!
"When will the new moon be over," you ask,
    "that we may sell our grain,
        and the sabbath, that we may display the wheat?
We will diminish the ephah,
    add to the shekel,
        and fix our scales for cheating!
We will **buy the lowly** for silver,
    and the poor for a pair of sandals;
        even the refuse of the wheat we will sell!"
The LORD has sworn by the pride of Jacob:
    Never will I forget a thing they have done!

The word of the Lord. **Thanks be to God.**

Responsorial Psalm (Psalm 113:1-2, 4-6, 7-8)

R. **Praise the Lord who lifts up the poor.** Or **Alleluia.**

Praise, you servants of the LORD,
    praise the name of the LORD.
Blessed be the name of the LORD
    both now and forever. R.

High above all nations is the LORD;
    above the heavens is his glory.
Who is like the, our God, who is enthroned on high
    and looks upon the heavens and the earth below? R.

He raises up the lowly from the dust;
    from the dunghill he lifts up the poor
to seat them with princes,
    with the princes of his own people. R.

Second Reading (1 Timothy 2:1-8)

Beloved: First of all, I ask that supplications, prayers, petitions, and thanksgivings be offered for everyone, for kings and for all in authority, that we may lead a quiet and tranquil life in all devotion and dignity. This is good and pleasing to God our savior, who wills everyone to be saved and to come to knowledge of the truth.

> For there is one God.
> There is also one **mediator** between God and men,
> the man Christ Jesus,
> who gave himself as ransom for all.

This was the testimony at the proper time. For this I was appointed preacher and **apostle**—I am speaking the truth, I am not lying—, teacher of the Gentiles in faith and truth.

It is my wish, then, that in every place the men should pray, lifting up holy hands, without anger or argument.

The word of the Lord. **Thanks be to God.**

Gospel (Luke 16:1-13 or 16:10-13)

The shorter version begins at the asterisks.

A reading from the holy Gospel according to Luke.
Glory to you, O Lord.

Jesus said to his disciples, "A rich man had a steward who was reported to him for squandering his property. He summoned him and said, 'What is this I hear about you? Prepare a full account of your stewardship, because you can no longer be my steward.' The steward said to himself, 'What shall I do, now that my master is taking the position of steward away from me? I am not strong enough to dig and I am ashamed to beg. I know what I shall do so that, when I am removed from the stewardship, they may welcome me into their homes.' He called in his master's debtors one by one. To the first he said, 'How much do you owe my master?' He replied, 'One hundred measures of olive oil.' He said to him, 'Here is your promissory note. Sit down and quickly write one for fifty.' Then to another the steward said, 'And you, how much do you owe?' He replied, 'One hundred kors of wheat.' The steward said to him, 'Here is your promissory note; write one for eighty.' And the master commended that dishonest steward for acting prudently. "For the children of this world are more prudent in dealing with their own generation than are the children of light. I tell you, make friends for yourselves with dishonest wealth, so that when it fails, you will be welcomed into eternal dwellings."

* * *

(Jesus said to his disciples:) "The person who is **trustworthy** in very small matters is also trustworthy in great ones; and the person who is dishonest in very small matters is also dishonest in great ones. If, therefore, you are not trustworthy with dishonest wealth, who will trust you with true wealth? If you are not trustworthy with what belongs to another, who will give you what is yours? No servant can serve two masters. He will either hate one and love the other, or be devoted to one and despise the other. You cannot serve both God and mammon."

The Gospel of the Lord. **Praise to you, Lord Jesus Christ.**

Key Words

Amos was a prophet and a friend of God. He lived 800 years before Jesus, at a time when rich people were very prosperous because they took advantage of the poor. The wealthy even bribed the judges. Amos spoke boldly to the rich and powerful, telling them this went against what God wanted.

. . . .

Buying the lowly, by making them sell their labor for wages so low that they cannot meet their basic needs, is taking advantage of them. God will not forget if his children are treated unjustly, for the Lord is a God of justice.

A **mediator** is someone who helps two people communicate in order to solve a dispute. Jesus, the Word of God, is our mediator so that humanity can encounter the true God without our human frailties getting in the way.

. . . .

Apostle is a Greek word for "a person who is sent." The apostles were the twelve followers chosen by Jesus. Saint Paul also considered himself to be an apostle, even though he did not meet Jesus while he was on earth. Rather, Saint Paul encountered the risen Jesus on the road to Damascus.

. . . .

To be **trustworthy** is to be honest and caring, diligently carrying out whatever task we have been given.

September 28
26th Sunday in Ordinary Time

First Reading (Amos 6:1a, 4-7)

Thus says the LORD the God of hosts:
Woe to the **complacent** in Zion!
Lying upon beds of ivory,
    stretched comfortably on their couches,
they eat lambs taken from the flock,
    and calves from the stall!
Improvising to the music of the harp,
    like David, they devise their own accompaniment.
They drink wine from bowls
    and anoint themselves with the best oils;
    yet they are not made ill by the collapse of Joseph!
Therefore, now they shall be the first to go into exile,
    and their wanton **revelry** shall be done away with.

The word of the Lord. **Thanks be to God.**

Responsorial Psalm (Psalm 146:7, 8-9, 9-10)

R. **Praise the Lord, my soul! Or Alleluia.**

Blessed he who keeps faith forever,
    secures justice for the oppressed,
    gives food to the hungry.
The LORD sets captives free. R.

The LORD gives sight to the blind.
    The LORD raises up those who were bowed down.
The LORD loves the just;
    the LORD protects strangers. R.

The fatherless and the widow he sustains,
    but the way of the wicked he thwarts.
The LORD shall reign forever;
    your God, O Zion, through all generations. Alleluia. R.

Second Reading (1 Timothy 6:11-16)

But you, man of God, pursue righteousness, devotion, faith, love, patience, and **gentleness**. Compete well for the faith. Lay hold of eternal life, to which you were called when you made the noble confession in the presence of many witnesses. I charge you before God, who gives life to all things, and before Christ Jesus, who gave testimony under Pontius Pilate for the noble confession, to keep the commandment without stain or reproach until the appearance of our Lord Jesus Christ that the blessed and only ruler will make manifest at the proper time, the King of kings and Lord of lords, who alone has immortality, who dwells in **unapproachable light**, and whom no human being has seen or can see. To him be honor and eternal power. Amen.

The word of the Lord. **Thanks be to God.**

Gospel (Luke 16:19-31)

A reading from the holy Gospel according to Luke.
Glory to you, O Lord.

Jesus said to the Pharisees: "There was a rich man who dressed in purple garments and fine linen and dined sumptuously each day. And lying at his door was a poor man named **Lazarus**, covered with sores, who would gladly have eaten his fill of the scraps that fell from the rich man's table. Dogs even used to come and lick his sores. When the poor man died, he was carried away by angels to the bosom of Abraham. The rich man also died and was buried, and from the netherworld, where he was in torment, he raised his eyes and saw Abraham far off and Lazarus at his side. And he cried out, 'Father Abraham, have pity on me. Send Lazarus to dip the tip of his finger in water and cool my tongue, for I am suffering torment in these flames.' Abraham replied, 'My child, remember that you received what was good during your lifetime while Lazarus likewise received what was bad; but now he is comforted here, whereas you are tormented. Moreover, between us and you a great chasm is established to prevent anyone from crossing who might wish to go from our side to yours or from your side to ours.' He said, 'Then I beg you, father, send him to my father's house, for I have five brothers, so that he may warn them, lest they too come to this place of torment.' But Abraham replied, 'They have Moses and the prophets. Let them listen to them.' He said, 'Oh no, father Abraham, but if someone from the dead goes to them, they will repent.' Then Abraham said, 'If they will not listen to Moses and the prophets, neither will they be persuaded if someone should rise from the dead.' "

The Gospel of the Lord. **Praise to you, Lord Jesus Christ.**

Key Words

Woe to are words that mean "too bad" or "shame." It is a way of saying things are not going to turn out well.

The Prophet Amos warns the rich that they have become **complacent,** which means they have hardened their hearts. They are not grieved: they do not see the suffering and decay around them; they do not feel anything.

Revelry means celebrating and having a good time. Amos warns the rich that their days of thinking only of themselves and their own pleasure are over; their wealth will not protect them from the justice of the Lord.

The call to **gentleness** is a call to respond without aggression when we are offended and humiliated. We must not act hastily, but with thought and care.

Saint Paul compares the mystery of God to a light so powerful and bright that we can't stare at it — it is an **unapproachable light.** Even if we spend all our lives, we can never fully learn all there is to know about God.

In this parable, there is a man named **Lazarus.** He is poor and diseased and he is ignored by the rich man by whose gate he rests. Note that the rich man is not named in this parable. The name "Lazarus" means "one whom God has helped." There is also a man named Lazarus in the Gospel of John; he is the brother of Martha and Mary and the one whom Jesus brought back from the dead.

October 5
27th Sunday in Ordinary Time

First Reading (Habakkuk 1:2-3; 2:2-4)

How long, O Lord? I cry for help
but **you do not listen**!
I cry out to you, "Violence!"
but you do not intervene.
Why do you let me see ruin;
why must I look at misery?
Destruction and violence are before me;
there is strife, and clamorous discord.
Then the Lord answered me and said:
Write down the vision clearly upon the tablets,
so that one can read it readily.
For the vision still has its time,
presses on to fulfillment, and will not disappoint;
if it delays, wait for it,
it will surely come, it will not be late.
The rash one has no integrity;
but the just one, because of his faith, shall live.

The word of the Lord. **Thanks be to God.**

Responsorial Psalm (Psalm 95:1-2, 6-7, 8-9)

R. **If today you hear his voice, harden not your hearts.**

Come, let us sing joyfully to the Lord;
let us acclaim the Rock of our salvation.
Let us come into his presence with thanksgiving;
let us joyfully sing psalms to him. R.

Come, let us **bow down** in worship;
let us kneel before the Lord who made us.
For he is our God,
and we are the people he shepherds,
the flock he guides. R.

Oh, that today you would hear his voice:
"Harden not your hearts as at Meribah,
as in the day of Massah in the desert,
where your fathers tempted me;
they tested me though they had seen my works." R.

Second Reading (2 Timothy 1:6-8, 13-14)

Beloved: I remind you, to stir into flame the gift of God that you have through the **imposition of my hands**. For God did not give us a spirit of cowardice but rather of power and love and **self-control**. So do not be ashamed of your **testimony** to our Lord, nor of me, a prisoner for his sake; but bear your share of hardship for the gospel with the strength that comes from God.

Take as your norm the sound words that you heard from me, in the faith and love that are in Christ Jesus. Guard this rich trust with the help of the Holy Spirit that dwells within us.

The word of the Lord. **Thanks be to God.**

Gospel (Luke 17:5-10)

A reading from the holy Gospel according to Luke.
Glory to you, O Lord.

The apostles said to the Lord, "**Increase our faith**." The Lord replied, "If you have faith the size of a mustard seed, you would say to this mulberry tree, 'Be uprooted and planted in the sea,' and it would obey you.

"Who among you would say to your servant who has just come in from plowing or tending sheep in the field, 'Come here immediately and take your place at table'? Would he not rather say to him, 'Prepare something for me to eat. Put on your apron and wait on me while I eat and drink. You may eat and drink when I am finished'? Is he grateful to that servant because he did what was commanded? So should it be with you. When you have done all you have been commanded, say, 'We are unprofitable servants; we have done what we were obliged to do.'"

The Gospel of the Lord.
Praise to you, Lord Jesus Christ.

Key Words

Habakkuk was a prophet who lived at the end of the seventh century before Christ. He was an unusual prophet, because he openly questioned the wisdom of God when he saw all the suffering endured by God's people.

Habakkuk complained to God, **"You do not listen"** — a bold thing to say. Habakkuk, nevertheless, taught the people to hope in God and believe in God's promises. He believed God was with him and he continued to pray until God responded with a message of hope.

When we **bow down,** we adopt a posture that shows reverence toward God. It is a way for us to acknowledge that we are before our Creator and Lord. When we enter a church, we bow or genuflect as a sign of reverence.

The **imposition of hands** was a gesture used by Saint Paul and other apostles in order to pass on the Holy Spirit to new Christians. This gesture is still used when priests are ordained, in the sacrament of confirmation, and when we pray over the sick.

A person exercises **self-control** when they learn to use all things without excess. We can, for example, eat, have fun, relax — but in moderation. This way, we honor God's gifts without bringing harm to ourselves or others.

A **testimony** is a word or example given so that others may be convinced of something. For example, the martyrs were Christians who offered their lives in testimony, or witness, so that others would believe in Jesus.

The apostles asked Jesus to **"increase our faith."** Our faith is a gift from God that will increase through prayer, study, the sacraments, and love of our neighbor.

October 12
28th Sunday in Ordinary Time

First Reading (2 Kings 5:14-17)

Naaman went down and plunged into the Jordan seven times at the word of Elisha, the man of God. His flesh became again like the flesh of a little child, and he was clean of his leprosy.

Naaman returned with his whole retinue to the man of God. On his arrival he stood before Elisha and said, "Now I know that there is no God in all the earth, except in Israel. Please accept a gift from your servant."

Elisha replied, "As the LORD lives whom I serve, I will not take it;" and despite Naaman's urging, he still refused. Naaman said: "If you will not accept, please let me, your servant, have two mule-loads of earth, for I will no longer offer holocaust or sacrifice to any other god except to the LORD."

The word of the Lord. **Thanks be to God.**

Responsorial Psalm (Psalm 98:1, 2-3, 3-4)

R. **The Lord has revealed to the nations his saving power.**

Sing to the LORD new song,
    for he has done wondrous deeds;
his right hand has won victory for him,
    his holy arm. R.

The LORD has made his salvation known:
    in the sight of the nations he has revealed his justice.
He has remembered his kindness and his faithfulness
    toward the house of Israel. R.

All the ends of the earth have seen
    the salvation by our God.
Sing joyfully to the LORD, all you lands:
    break into song; sing praise. R.

Second Reading (2 Timothy 2:8-13)

Beloved: Remember Jesus Christ, raised from the dead, a descendant of **David**: such is my **gospel**, for which I am suffering, even to the point of chains, like a criminal. But the word of God is not chained. Therefore, I bear with everything for the sake of those who are chosen, so that they too may obtain the salvation that is in Christ Jesus, together with eternal glory. This saying is trustworthy:

> If we have died with him
> > we shall also live with him;
> if we persevere
> > we shall also reign with him.
> But if we deny him
> > he will deny us.
> If we are unfaithful
> > he remains faithful,
> > for he cannot deny himself.

The word of the Lord. **Thanks be to God.**

Gospel (Luke 17:11-19)

A reading from the holy Gospel according to Luke.
Glory to you, O Lord.

As Jesus continued his journey to Jerusalem, he traveled through Samaria and Galilee. As he was entering a village, ten lepers met him. They **stood at a distance** from him and raised their voices, saying, "Jesus, Master! Have pity on us!" And when he saw them, he said, "Go show yourselves to the **priests**." As they were going they were cleansed. And one of them, realizing he had been healed, returned, glorifying God in a loud voice; and he fell at the feet of Jesus and thanked him. He was a **Samaritan**. Jesus said in reply, "Ten were cleansed, were they not? Where are the other nine? Has none but this foreigner returned to give thanks to God?" Then he said to him, "Stand up and go; your faith has saved you."

The Gospel of the Lord. **Praise to you, Lord Jesus Christ.**

Key Words

In the Bible, the two books of **Kings** tell the story of a time when Israel was ruled by kings. The books begin with the death of King David, nearly 1,000 years before Jesus was born, and end when the Babylonians capture Jerusalem, nearly 600 years before Jesus. The writer wants us to see how God helped his people throughout history.

. . . .

David was the second king of Israel, from the year 1010 to 970 before Christ. David was said to have musical talent and was the hero who killed the giant Goliath. Although he committed serious errors a few times during his reign, in all, he was a good king, well-loved by the people.

. . . .

The word **gospel** means a message that communicates good news. There are four gospels in the Bible, written by Saints Matthew, Mark, Luke, and John. The word "gospel" also means the good news that Jesus rose from the dead.

People who suffered from Hansen's disease, or leprosy, were told to **stand at a distance** from healthy people, who believed they would become infected if the sick came too near. This meant that lepers had to live far outside the village limits.

. . . .

Lepers who believed they were cured had to show themselves to the **priests** so that they could be assured they were healthy again. The priests would decide whether they could return to live among the people.

. . . .

Samaritans were people who came from Samaria, a region of Israel to the south of Galilee and to the north of Judea. Jews and Samaritans did not talk to each other because of historical differences. It is astonishing that the only leper to say thank you to Jesus was a Samaritan.

October 19

29th Sunday in Ordinary Time

First Reading (Exodus 17:8-13)

In those days, **Amalek** came and waged war against Israel. Moses, therefore, said to Joshua, "Pick out certain men, and tomorrow go out and engage Amalek in battle. I will be standing on top of the hill with the **staff** of God in my hand." So Joshua did as Moses told him: he engaged Amalek in battle after Moses had climbed to the top of the hill with Aaron and Hur. As long as Moses kept his hands raised up, Israel had the better of the fight, but when he let his hands rest, Amalek had the better of the fight. Moses' hands, however, grew tired; so they put a rock in place for him to sit on. Meanwhile Aaron and Hur supported his hands, one on one side and one on the other, so that his hands remained steady till sunset. And Joshua mowed down Amalek and his people with the edge of the sword.

The word of the Lord. **Thanks be to God.**

Responsorial Psalm (Psalm 121:1-2, 3-4, 5-6, 7-8)

R. **Our help is from the Lord, who made heaven and earth.**

I lift up my eyes toward the mountains;
 whence shall help come to me?
My help is from the LORD,
 who made heaven and earth. R.

May he not suffer your foot to slip;
 may he slumber not who guards you:
indeed he neither slumbers nor sleeps,
 the guardian of Israel. R.

The LORD is your guardian; the LORD is your shade;
 he is beside you at your right hand.
The sun shall not harm you by day,
 nor the moon by night. R.

The LORD will guard you from all evil;
 he will guard your life.
The LORD will guard your coming and your going,
 both now and forever. R.

Second Reading (2 Timothy 3:14–4:2)

Beloved: Remain faithful to what you have learned and believed, because you know from whom you learned it, and that from infancy you have known the sacred Scriptures, which are capable of giving you wisdom for salvation through faith in Christ Jesus. All Scripture is inspired by God and is useful for teaching, for refutation, for correction, and for training in righteousness, so that one who belongs to God may be competent, equipped for every good work.

I charge you in the presence of God and of Christ Jesus, who will judge the living and the dead, and by his **appearing** and his kingly power: proclaim the word; be persistent whether it is convenient or inconvenient; convince, reprimand, encourage through all patience and teaching.

The word of the Lord. **Thanks be to God.**

Gospel (Luke 18:1-8)

A reading from the holy Gospel according to Luke.
Glory to you, O Lord.

Jesus told his disciples a parable about the necessity for them to pray always without becoming weary. He said, "There was a judge in a certain town who neither feared God nor respected any human being. And a **widow** in that town used to come to him and say, 'Render a just decision for me against my adversary.' For a long time the judge was unwilling, but eventually he thought, 'While it is true that I neither fear God nor respect any human being, because this widow keeps bothering me I shall deliver a just decision for her lest she finally come and strike me.' " The Lord said, "Pay attention to what the dishonest judge says. Will not God then secure the rights of his chosen ones who call out to him day and night? Will he be slow to answer them? I tell you, he will see to it that justice is done for them speedily. But when the Son of Man comes, will he find faith on earth?"

The Gospel of the Lord. **Praise to you, Lord Jesus Christ.**

The Amalekites were a tribe led by **Amalek** that lived to the south of Palestine. Although they were descended from Abraham, they were long-time enemies of Israel. The Israelites had to conquer them in order to reach the Promised Land.

The **staff** of God was a sign of the authority that Moses had over the people of Israel. In our times, we still use similar symbols to show that God has given a person the authority to help others. The Pope and bishops, for example, in some ceremonies use the crozier (a tall staff) as a sign that they are shepherds who guide us Christians.

Timothy was a companion of Saint Paul. He helped Paul to spread the gospel and at one time was thrown into jail with his master. In the New Testament, there are two letters to Timothy, where Saint Paul gives him advice as the person responsible for the Church in Ephesus.

Jesus is always with us when we gather in community, when we read the word of God, when we celebrate the Eucharist, and when we help someone who is in need. Nevertheless, Saint Paul and the early Christians yearned for the **appearing** of Christ among them. Jesus promised that he would come back to us in a visible way, at the end of time when history reaches its fulfillment.

A **widow** is a woman whose husband has died. At the time of Jesus, when she married her husband, she left her own family and became part of her husband's family. When he died, she was left without anyone to care for her or protect her, leaving her among the poor and powerless of the community.

October 26
30th Sunday in Ordinary Time

First Reading (Sirach 35:12-14, 16-18)

The LORD is a God of justice,
who knows no **favorites**.
Though not unduly partial toward the weak,
   yet he hears the cry of the oppressed.
The Lord is not deaf to the wail of the orphan,
   nor to the widow when she pours out her complaint.
The one who serves God willingly is heard;
   his petition reaches the heavens.
The prayer of the lowly pierces the clouds;
   it does not **rest** till it reaches its goal,
nor will it withdraw till the Most High responds,
   judges justly and affirms the right,
and the Lord will not delay.

The word of the Lord. **Thanks be to God.**

Responsorial Psalm (Psalm 34:2-3, 17-18, 19, 23)

R. **The Lord hears the cry of the poor.**

I will bless the LORD at all times;
   his praise shall be ever in my mouth.
Let my soul glory in the LORD;
   the lowly will hear me and be glad. R.

The LORD confronts the evildoers,
   to destroy remembrance of them from the earth.
When the just cry out, the LORD hears them,
   and from all their distress he rescues them. R.

The LORD is close to the brokenhearted;
   and those who are crushed in spirit he saves.
The LORD redeems the lives of his servants;
   no one incurs guilt who takes refuge in him. R.

Second Reading (2 Timothy 4:6-8, 16-18)

Beloved: I am already being poured out like a **libation**, and the time of my departure is at hand. I have competed well; I have finished the race; I have kept the faith. From now on the crown of righteousness awaits me, which the Lord, the just judge, will award to me on that day, and not only to me, but to all who have longed for his appearance.

At my first defense no one appeared on my behalf, but everyone deserted me. May it not be held against them! But the Lord stood by me and gave me strength, so that through me the proclamation might be completed and all the Gentiles might hear it. And I was rescued from the lion's mouth. The Lord will rescue me from every evil threat and will bring me safe to his heavenly kingdom. To him be glory forever and ever. Amen.

The word of the Lord. **Thanks be to God.**

Gospel (Luke 18:9-14)

A reading from the holy Gospel according to Luke.
Glory to you, O Lord.

Jesus addressed this parable to those who were convinced of their own righteousness and despised everyone else. "Two people went up to the temple area to pray; one was a Pharisee and the other was a tax collector. The Pharisee took up his position and spoke this prayer to himself, 'O God, I thank you that I am not like the rest of humanity—greedy, dishonest, adulterous—or even like this tax collector. I fast twice a week, and I pay **tithes** on my whole income.' But the tax collector stood off at a distance and would not even raise his eyes to heaven but beat his breast and prayed, 'O God, be merciful to me a sinner.' I tell you, the latter went home justified, not the former; for whoever **exalts** himself will be humbled, and the one who humbles himself will be exalted."

The Gospel of the Lord. **Praise to you, Lord Jesus Christ.**

Key Words

A judge is someone who is called to know no **favorites,** that is, without showing favor but treating everyone equally and with fairness. Sirach believes God to be a just and fair judge.

To **rest** is to stop or hold back from doing something. We are reminded to be persistent in our prayer and not to grow tired in bringing to God our needs and cares.

A **libation** is a special drink that is poured out as a way to honor a god. Saint Paul uses this wonderful image to describe his life in service of the gospel — he is pouring his life out as an offering to God.

The people of Israel were required to give a tenth of their earnings, whether in produce or money, to support the temple as well as the poor. This ancient practice is known as **tithing** (from the Old English word for 'tenth'). Today, many people set aside one-tenth of their income for charity as a form of tithing.

To **exalt** someone is to praise or elevate them to a high level. In today's parable, Jesus cautions against exalting ourselves or being overly proud of ourselves. True humility is our proper stance before God.

First Reading (Revelation 7:2-4, 9-14)

I, John, saw another angel come up from the East, holding the seal of the living God. He cried out in a loud voice to the four angels who were given power to damage the land and the sea, "Do not damage the land or the sea or the trees until we put the seal on the foreheads of the servants of our God." I heard the number of those who had been marked with the seal, one hundred and forty-four thousand marked from every tribe of the children of Israel.

After this I had a vision of a great multitude, which no one could count, from every nation, race, people, and tongue. They stood before the throne and before the Lamb, wearing white robes and holding palm branches in their hands. They cried out in a loud voice:

"Salvation comes from our God, who is seated on the throne,
    and from the Lamb."

All the angels stood around the throne and around the elders and the four living creatures. They prostrated themselves before the throne, worshiped God, and exclaimed:

"Amen. Blessing and glory, wisdom and thanksgiving,
    honor, power, and might
be to our God forever and ever. Amen."

Then one of the elders spoke up and said to me, "Who are these **wearing white robes**, and where did they come from?" I said to him, "My lord, you are the one who knows." He said to me, "These are the ones who have survived the time of great distress; they have washed their robes and made them white in the Blood of the Lamb."

The word of the Lord. **Thanks be to God.**

Responsorial Psalm (Psalm 24:1bc-2, 3-4ab, 5-6)

R. **Lord, this is the people that longs to see your face.**

The LORD's are the earth and its fullness;
    the world and those who dwell in it.
For he founded it upon the seas
    and established it upon the rivers. R.

Who can ascend the mountain of the LORD?
>or who may stand in his holy place?
One whose hands are sinless, whose heart is clean,
>who desires not what is vain. R.

He shall receive a blessing from the LORD,
a reward from God his savior.
Such is the race that seeks him,
that seeks the face of the God of Jacob. R.

Second Reading (1 John 3:1-3)

Beloved: See what love the Father has bestowed on us that we may be called the children of God. Yet so we are. The reason the world does not know us is that it did not know him. Beloved, we are God's children now; what we shall be has not yet been revealed. We do know that when it is revealed we shall be like him, for we shall see him as he is. Everyone who has this hope based on him makes himself pure, as he is pure.

The word of the Lord. **Thanks be to God.**

Gospel (Matthew 5:1-12a)

A reading from the holy Gospel according to Matthew.
Glory to you, O Lord.

When Jesus saw the crowds, he went **up the mountain**, and after he had sat down, his disciples came to him. He began to teach them, saying:

"Blessed are the poor in spirit,
>for theirs is the Kingdom of heaven.
Blessed are they who mourn,
>for they will be comforted.
Blessed are the meek,
>for they will inherit the land.
Blessed are they who hunger and thirst for righteousness,
>for they will be satisfied.
Blessed are the merciful,
>for they will be shown mercy.
Blessed are the clean of heart,
>for they will see God.

Blessed are the peacemakers,
for they will be called children of God.
Blessed are they who are persecuted for the sake
of righteousness,
for theirs is the Kingdom of heaven.

Blessed are you when they insult you and persecute you and utter every kind of evil against you falsely because of me. Rejoice and be glad, for your reward will be great in heaven."

The Gospel of the Lord. **Praise to you, Lord Jesus Christ.**

Key Words

All Saints is the day when we remember all the saints who live with God in heaven. This includes all the men and women we officially call saints but also all the holy people whose sainthood is known only by God.

The **Book of Revelation** is the last book of the Bible. Its messages are hidden in symbols that often seem very strange to us. Everything has a hidden meaning—the colors, numbers, even the dragons and monsters. The early Christians understood what the writer was trying to tell them. They were facing difficult times, but Revelation told them not to be discouraged, for in the end, Jesus would win over all their enemies.

Those **wearing white robes** are the ones who belong to Jesus. When you were baptized, you were dressed in a white garment to show that you too are part of his people.

Just as Moses went **up the mountain** to get the Ten Commandments from God, Jesus goes up the mountain to proclaim his beatitudes ("Blessed are..."). These beatitudes show us how to live today and help us move even more deeply into God's love.

November 2
The Commemoration of All the Faithful Departed (All Souls' Day)

First Reading (Wisdom 3:1-9)

The **souls of the just** are in the hand of God,
  and no torment shall touch them.
They seemed, in the view of the foolish, to be dead;
  and their passing away was thought an affliction
  and their going forth from us, utter destruction.
But they are in peace.
For if before men, indeed, they be punished,
  yet is their hope full of immortality;
chastised a little, they shall be greatly blessed,
  because God tried them
  and found them worthy of himself.
As gold in the furnace, he proved them,
  and as sacrificial offerings he took them to himself.
In the time of their visitation they shall shine,
  and shall dart about as sparks through stubble;
they shall judge nations and rule over peoples,
  and the LORD shall be their King forever.
Those who trust in him shall understand truth,
  and the faithful shall abide with him in love:
because **grace and mercy** are with his holy ones,
  and his care is with his elect.

The word of the Lord. **Thanks be to God.**

Responsorial Psalm (Psalm 23:1b-3a, 3b-4, 5, 6)

R. **The Lord is my shepherd; there is nothing I shall want.**
Or Though I walk in the valley of darkness, I fear no evil, for you are with me.

The LORD is my shepherd; I shall not want.
  In verdant pastures he gives me repose;
beside restful waters he leads me;
  he refreshes my soul. R.

He guides me in right paths
  for his name's sake.
Even though I walk in the dark valley
  I fear no evil; for you are at my side
with your rod and your staff
  that give me courage. R.

You spread the table before me
in the sight of my foes;
You anoint my head with oil;
my cup overflows. R.

Only goodness and kindness follow me
all the days of my life;
and I shall dwell in the house of the LORD
for years to come. R.

Second Reading (Romans 5:5-11 or Romans 6:3-9)

Brothers and sisters:
Hope does not disappoint,
because the love of God has been poured out into our hearts
through the Holy Spirit that has been given to us.
For Christ, while we were still helpless,
died at the appointed time for the ungodly.
Indeed, only with difficulty does one die for a just person,
though perhaps for a good person
one might even find courage to die.
But God proves his love for us
in that while we were still sinners Christ died for us.
How much more then, since we are now justified by his Blood,
will we be saved through him from the wrath.
Indeed, if, while we were enemies,
we were reconciled to God through the death of his Son,
how much more, once reconciled,
will we be saved by his life.
Not only that,
but we also boast of God through our Lord Jesus Christ,
through whom we have now received **reconciliation**.

The word of the Lord. **Thanks be to God.**

Gospel (John 6:37-40)

Jesus said to the crowds:
"Everything that the Father gives me will come to me,
and I will not reject anyone who comes to me,
because I **came down from heaven** not to do my own will
but the will of the one who sent me.
And this is the will of the one who sent me,
that I should not lose anything of what he gave me,
but that I should raise it on the last day.
For this is the will of my Father,
that everyone who sees the Son and believes in him
may have **eternal life**,
and I shall raise him on the last day."

The Gospel of the Lord. **Praise to you, Lord Jesus Christ.**

The **souls of the just** are those who have lived a life in communion with God's commandments and have turned from sin. They have become saints. Every person has both a body and a soul. By loving God and closely following the teachings of Jesus, we can be with the souls of the just in heaven some day.

God's **grace and mercy** are always available to us. Whenever we stray from the teachings of the Church, God always wants us back. We do not need to be afraid to admit our faults. As long as we are sorry for having sinned, and we do our best to sin no more, we are welcomed to enjoy God's eternal love.

Just like the people in Saint Paul's time, we are called to **reconciliation.** That's a big word for fixing a relationship that has been damaged. Jesus helps us to fix our problems.

John's gospel today tells the story of Jesus speaking to the crowds with important messages. Jesus tells them something that is very hard for them to believe...that he **"came down from heaven."** to do his Father's will (what God has asked him to do). When we honor our father and mother by being obedient, we are also doing God's will.

One of the greatest messages in the gospels is that we have been lovingly created by God to live forever! **Eternal life** means that we will be raised to new life after our time here on earth. As members of the faith, we know that we can live forever if we do God's will. We are told by Jesus that we should treat our neighbors, and even our "enemies," as we would want to be treated. Even as we travel through our earthly life, we can experience a taste of the joy that awaits us in heaven.

First Reading (Ezekiel 47:1-2, 8-9, 12)

The angel brought me
  back to the entrance of the temple,
  and I saw **water flowing out**
  from beneath the threshold of the temple toward the east,
  for the façade of the temple was toward the east;
  the water flowed down from the southern side of the temple,
  south of the altar.
He led me outside by the north gate,
  and around to the outer gate facing the east,
  where I saw water trickling from the southern side.
He said to me,
"This water flows into the eastern district down upon the Arabah,
  and empties into the sea, the salt waters, which it makes fresh.
Wherever the river flows,
  every sort of living creature that can multiply shall live,
  and there shall be abundant fish,
  for wherever this water comes the sea shall be made fresh.
Along both banks of the river, fruit trees of every kind shall grow;
  their leaves shall not fade, nor their fruit fail.
Every month they shall bear fresh fruit,
  for they shall be watered by the flow from the sanctuary.
Their fruit shall serve for food, and their leaves for medicine."

The word of the Lord. **Thanks be to God.**

Responsorial Psalm (Psalm 46:2-3, 5-6, 8-9)

R. **The waters of the river gladden the city of God,
the holy dwelling of the Most High!**

God is our refuge and our strength,
  an ever-present help in distress.
Therefore, we fear not, though the earth be shaken
  and mountains plunge into the depths of the sea. R.

There is a stream whose runlets gladden the city of God,
  the holy dwelling of the Most High.
God is in its midst; it shall not be disturbed;
  God will help it at the break of dawn. R.

The LORD of hosts is with us;
    our **stronghold** is the God of Jacob.
Come! behold the deeds of the Lord,
    the astounding things he has wrought on earth. R.

Second Reading (1 Corinthians 3:9c-11, 16-17)

Brothers and sisters:
You are God's building.
According to the grace of God given to me,
    like a wise master builder I laid a foundation,
    and another is building upon it.
But each one must be careful how he builds upon it,
    for no one can lay a foundation other than the one that is there,
    namely, Jesus Christ.
Do you not know that you are the temple of God,
    and that the Spirit of God dwells in you?
If anyone destroys God's temple,
    God will destroy that person;
    for the temple of God, which you are, is holy.

The word of the Lord. **Thanks be to God.**

Gospel (John 2:13-22)

Since the Passover of the Jews was near,
Jesus went up to Jerusalem.
He found in the temple area those who sold oxen, sheep, and doves,
    as well as the money-changers seated there.
He made a whip out of cords
    and drove them all out of the temple area,
        with the sheep and oxen,
    and spilled the coins of the money-changers
    and overturned their tables,
    and to those who sold doves he said,
"Take these out of here,
    and stop making my Father's house a marketplace."
His disciples recalled the words of Scripture,
    Zeal for your house will consume me.
At this the Jews answered and said to him,
    "What sign can you show us for doing this?"
Jesus answered and said to them,
    "Destroy this temple and in three days I will raise it up."
The Jews said,
    "This temple has been under construction for forty-six years,
    and you will raise it up in three days?"
But he was speaking about the temple of his Body.
Therefore, when he was raised from the dead,
    his disciples remembered that he had said this,
    and they came to believe the Scripture
    and the word Jesus had spoken.

The Gospel of the Lord. **Praise to you, Lord Jesus Christ.**

Key Words

The **water flowing out** is a symbol for many things, especially new life. When we are baptized, we are baptized into new life through water and the Spirit. The water in our First Reading flows from the temple and creates life wherever it goes. As humans, we cannot live without water. It keeps us alive, but also keeps us clean. We are also washed clean when we take part in the sacrament of reconciliation.

. . . .

A **stronghold** is a secure place. Some might call it a refuge or a place where you could survive an attack. It was very important in biblical times to have a stronghold since wars and battles were common. A safe place to prepare for an attack meant that you could defend yourself much better. God is our refuge and our stronghold against the dangers of the world.

Saint Paul, who wrote the letter to the **Corinthians**, our second reading today, was himself a convert to the faith. The Corinthians were members of the Church in Corinth. Paul is telling them that God loves them and that they are holy. Each of us are holy. We each are a temple of God.

. . . .

The story in today's gospel shows that Jesus was angry. Anger is not something that we usually think of when we think of Jesus. But Jesus did fight against injustices. He was angry that his father's house, the temple, was being used for evil purposes. When he says **"Destroy this temple** and in three days I will raise it up." the people do not understand. Many may have thought that he was not thinking clearly. But he was referring to his body, his death and resurrection. Our body, too, is a temple and we are called to take good care of it.

November 16
33rd Sunday in Ordinary Time

First Reading (Malachi 3:19-20a)

Lo, **the day is coming**, blazing like an oven,
> when all the proud and all evildoers will be stubble,
and the day that is coming will set them on fire,
> leaving them neither root nor branch,
> says the **LORD of hosts**.
But for you who fear my name, there will arise
> the sun of justice with its healing rays.

The word of the Lord. **Thanks be to God.**

Responsorial Psalm (Psalm 98:5-6, 7-8, 9)

R. **The Lord comes to rule the earth with justice.**

Sing praise to the LORD with the harp,
> with the harp and melodious song.
With trumpets and the sound of the horn
> sing joyfully before the King, the LORD. R.

Let the sea and what fills it resound,
> the world and those who dwell in it;
let the rivers clap their hands,
> the mountains shout with them for joy. R.

Before the LORD, for he comes,
> for he comes to rule the earth,
He will rule the world with justice
> and the peoples with equity. R.

Second Reading (2 Thessalonians 3:7-12)

Brothers and sisters: You know how one must imitate us. For we did not act in a disorderly way among you, nor did we eat food received free from anyone. On the contrary, in toil and drudgery, night and day we worked, so as not to burden any of you. Not that we do not have the right. Rather, we wanted to present ourselves as a model for you, so that you might imitate us. In fact, when we were with you, we instructed you that if anyone was unwilling to work, neither should that one eat. We hear that some are conducting themselves among you in a disorderly way, by not keeping busy but minding the business of others. Such people we instruct and urge in the Lord Jesus Christ to work quietly and to eat their own food.

The word of the Lord. **Thanks be to God.**

Gospel (Luke 21:5-19)

A reading from the holy Gospel according to Luke.
Glory to you, O Lord.

While some people were speaking about how the temple was adorned with costly stones and votive offerings, Jesus said, "All that you see here—the days will come when there will not be left a stone upon another stone that will not be thrown down."

Then they asked him, "Teacher, when will this happen? And what sign will there be when all these things are about to happen?" He answered, "See that you not be deceived, for many will come in my name, saying, '**I am he**,' and 'The time has come.' Do not follow them! When you hear of wars and insurrections, do not be terrified; for such things must happen first, but it will not immediately be the end." Then he said to them, "Nation will rise against nation, and kingdom against kingdom. There will be powerful earthquakes, famines, and plagues from place to place; and awesome sights and mighty signs will come from the sky.

"Before all this happens, however, they will seize and **persecute** you, they will hand you over to the synagogues and to prisons, and they will have you led before kings and governors because of my name. It will lead to your giving testimony. Remember, you are not to prepare your defense beforehand, for I myself shall give you a wisdom in speaking that all your adversaries will be powerless to resist or refute. You will even be handed over by parents, brothers, relatives, and friends, and they will put some of you to death. You will be hated by all because of my name, but **not a hair on your head will be destroyed**. By your perseverance you will secure your lives."

The Gospel of the Lord. **Praise to you, Lord Jesus Christ.**

Key Words

The phrase **"the day is coming"** refers to the last day of history at the end of time, when God will come to judge the living and the dead.

In the Bible, God is referred to as the **LORD of hosts** — a host being a large army or group. This title makes it clear that God is more powerful than all human power. He is master and Lord of all.

The **Gospel according to Luke** was written for Christians who were not Jewish. It is also known as the Gospel of mercy. Saint Luke wrote the Acts of the Apostles as well.

We are warned not to believe those who say, **"I am he!"** or to be led astray by others who would have us believe that they can save us. There is only one Savior and Lord, Jesus Christ.

At the time Saint Luke wrote his gospel, the early Christians were being **persecuted**, or oppressed, because of their faith in Jesus. Luke sought to give them hope at a difficult time.

Jesus made a promise to his followers that **"not a hair on your head will be destroyed."** This means that although we may pass through difficult moments, and although many Christians have lost their lives for the cause of the faith (such as the martyrs), nothing can happen that will lessen the love God has for us.

November 23
Our Lord Jesus Christ, King of the Universe (Christ the King)

First Reading (2 Samuel 5:1-3)

In those days, all the **tribes of Israel** came to David in Hebron and said: "Here we are, your bone and your flesh. In days past, when Saul was our king, it was you who led the Israelites out and brought them back. And the Lord said to you, 'You shall shepherd my people Israel and shall be commander of Israel.' " When all the elders of Israel came to David in Hebron, King David made an agreement with them there before the Lord, and they **anointed him king** of Israel.

The word of the Lord. **Thanks be to God.**

Responsorial Psalm (Psalm 122:1-2, 3-4, 4-5)

R. **Let us go rejoicing to the house of the Lord.**

I rejoiced because they said to me,
    "We will go up to the house of the LORD."
And now we have set foot
    within your gates, O Jerusalem. R.

Jerusalem, built as a city
    with compact unity.
To it the tribes go up,
    the tribes of the LORD. R.

According to the decree for Israel,
    to give thanks to the name of the LORD.
In it are set up judgment seats,
    seats for the house of David. R.

Second Reading (Colossians 1:12-20)

Brothers and sisters: Let us give thanks to the Father, who has made you fit to share in the inheritance of the holy ones in light. He delivered us from the power of darkness and transferred us to the kingdom of his beloved Son, in whom we have redemption, the forgiveness of sins.

He is the image of the invisible God,
    the firstborn of all creation.

For in him were created all things in heaven and on earth,
    the visible and the invisible,
    whether thrones or dominions or principalities or powers;
    all things were created through him and for him.
He is before all things,
    and in him all things hold together.
He is the head of the body, the church.
He is the beginning, the firstborn from the dead,
    that in all things he himself might be preeminent.
For in him all the fullness was pleased to dwell,
    and through him to **reconcile** all things for him,
    making peace by the blood of his cross
    through him, whether those on earth or those in heaven.

The word of the Lord. **Thanks be to God.**

Gospel (Luke 23:35-43)

A reading from the holy Gospel according to Luke.
Glory to you, O Lord.

The rulers sneered at Jesus and said, "He saved others, let him save himself if he is the chosen one, the Christ of God." Even the soldiers jeered at him. As they approached to offer him wine they called out, "If you are **King of the Jews**, save yourself." Above him there was an inscription that read, "This is the King of the Jews."

Now one of the criminals hanging there reviled Jesus, saying, "Are you not the Christ? Save yourself and us." The other, however, rebuking him, said in reply, "Have you no fear of God, for you are subject to the same condemnation? And indeed, we have been condemned justly, for the sentence we received corresponds to our crimes, but this man has done nothing criminal." Then he said, "Jesus, remember me when you come into your kingdom." He replied to him, "Amen, I say to you, today you will be with me in Paradise."

The Gospel of the Lord. **Praise to you, Lord Jesus Christ.**

Key Words

The Solemnity of **Our Lord Jesus Christ, King of the Universe** (also known as Christ the King) brings the liturgical year to a close. It is like New Year's Eve, with a new liturgical year beginning next Sunday on the First Sunday of Advent.

The **tribes of Israel** were groups of families, or clans, descended from Jacob. Israel was formed by the union of twelve tribes each known by the name of their founder: Reuben, Simeon, Levi, Judah, Zebulun, Issachar, Dan, Gad, Asher, Naphtali, Joseph, and Benjamin.

The elders **anointed him king** by pouring oil over his head in a ceremony in front of all the people. The new king, Jesus, is named "the anointed one" (the Christ) because, after he rose from the dead, his disciples realized that he was the true king.

Saint Paul wrote a letter to the **Colossians,** members of a Christian community in the town of Colossae (in modern-day Turkey). They were doubting their faith, but Paul's letter encouraged them to be strong and reminded them that Jesus comes before everything else.

By sin, humanity lost friendship with God, but because the Son of God was born to the Virgin Mary and died for our sins, God **reconciled** us to himself. Through the life, death, and resurrection of Jesus, we regained God's friendship.

On many crucifixes there is a small sign above Jesus with the letters INRI. These letters stand for Iesus Nazarenus Rex Iudaeorum which is Latin for "Jesus of Nazareth, **King of the Jews."**

Children's Prayers
for Various Occasions

A Child's Prayer for Morning

Now, before I run to play,
let me not forget to pray
to God who kept me through the night
and waked me with the morning light.

Help me, Lord, to love you more
than I have ever loved before.
In my work and in my play
please be with me through the day.
Amen.

Morning Prayer

Dear God, we thank you for this day.
We thank you for our families and friends.
We thank you for our classmates.
Be with us as we work and play today.
Help us always to be kind to each other.
We pray in the name of the Father,
and of the Son and of the Holy Spirit. Amen.

Heather Reid, *Let's Pray! Prayers for the Elementary
Classroom* (Ottawa: Novalis, 2006).

Angel of God

Angel of God, my guardian dear,
to whom God's love entrusts me here,
ever this day be at my side,
to light and guard, to rule and guide.
Amen.

Children's Bedtime Prayer

Now I lay me down to sleep,
I pray you, Lord, your child to keep.
Your love will guard me through the night
and wake me with the morning light. Amen.

Child's Evening Prayer

I hear no voice, I feel no touch,
I see no glory bright;
but yet I know that God is near,
in darkness as in light.

He watches ever by my side,
and hears my whispered prayer:
the Father for his little child
both night and day does care.

God Hear My Prayer

God in heaven hear my prayer,
keep me in your loving care.
Be my guide in all I do,
bless all those who love me too.
Amen.

Grace before Meals

Bless us, O Lord,
and these your gifts
which we are about to receive
from your bounty.
Through Christ our Lord. Amen.

* * *

For food in a world where many walk in hunger,
for friends in a world where many walk alone,
for faith in a world where many walk in fear,
we give you thanks, O God. Amen.

* * *

God is great, God is good!
Let us thank God for our food. Amen.

* * *

Be present at our table, Lord.
Be here and everywhere adored.
Your creatures bless
and grant that we may feast
in paradise with you. Amen.

Grace after Meals

We give you thanks, Almighty God,
for these and all the benefits we receive
from your bounty. Through Christ our Lord. Amen.

* * *

Blessed be the name of the Lord.
Now and forever. Amen.

THE ROSARY

In the Rosary we focus on 20 events or mysteries in the life and death of Jesus and meditate on how we share with Mary in the saving work of Christ. Reading a relevant passage from the Bible can help us to understand better a particular mystery of the Rosary. The Bible references below are suggestions; other biblical texts can also be used for meditation.

- Begin the Rosary at the crucifix by praying the Apostles' Creed.
- At each large bead, pray the Lord's Prayer. (back cover)
- At each small bead, pray the Hail Mary. (back cover)
- At the first three beads it is customary to pray a Hail Mary for each of the gifts of faith, hope, and love.
- For each mystery, begin with the Lord's Prayer, then recite the Hail Mary ten times, and end with Glory Be to the Father. (back cover)

The Five Joyful Mysteries:
The Annunciation (Luke 1.26-38)
The Visitation (Luke 1.39-56)
The Nativity (Luke 2.1-20)
The Presentation (Luke 2.22-38)
The Finding in the Temple (Luke 2.41-52)

The Five Mysteries of Light:
The Baptism in the Jordan (Matthew 3.13-17)
The Wedding at Cana (John 2.1-12)
The Proclamation of the Kingdom (Mark 1.15)
The Transfiguration (Luke 9.28-36)
The First Eucharist (Matthew 26.26-29)

The Five Sorrowful Mysteries:
The Agony in the Garden (Matthew 26.36-56)
The Scourging at the Pillar (Matthew 27.20-26)
The Crowning with Thorns (Matthew 27.27-30)
The Carrying of the Cross (Matthew 27.31-33)
The Crucifixion (Matthew 27.34-60)

The Five Glorious Mysteries:
The Resurrection (John 20.1-18)
The Ascension (Acts 1.9-11)
The Descent of the Holy Spirit (John 20.19-23)
The Assumption of Mary (John 11.26)
The Crowning of Mary (Philippians 2.1-11)

Prayer for Friends

Loving God, you are the best friend we can have.
We ask today that you help us to be good friends to
   each other.
Help us to be fair, kind and unselfish.
Keep our friends safe and happy.
Bless us and bless all friends in this community.
We pray in the name of Jesus,
who was always the friend of children. Amen.

Heather Reid, *Let's Pray! Prayers for the Elementary Classroom*
(Ottawa: Novalis, 2006).

In the Silence

If we really want to pray,
we must first learn to listen,
for in the silence of the heart,
God speaks.

Saint Teresa of Calcutta

Prayer for the Birthday Child

May God bless you with every
   good gift
and surround you with love and happiness.
May Jesus be your friend and guide
all the days of your life.
May the Spirit of God guide your footsteps
in the path of truth. Amen.

Prayer for Pets

Dear Father, hear and bless
your beasts and singing birds,
and guard with care and tenderness
small things that have no words. Amen.

OCCASIONAL PRAYERS

When Someone Has Died

Lord God, hear our cries.
Grant us comfort in our sadness,
gently wipe away our tears,
and give us courage in the days ahead.
We ask this through Christ our Lord. Amen.

Prayer for Student / Teacher Who Is Sick

Gracious God, _____ is sick right now. We pray for
(him/her/them) and ask that they get better quickly and be
able to return to us. Bless all nurses, doctors and everyone who
cares for people who are ill. May all sick people find comfort
through their families and friends. We ask this in the name of
Jesus, who healed many people. Amen.

Heather Reid, *Let's Pray: Prayers for the Elementary Classroom*
(Ottawa: Novalis, 2007).

Prayer for When I Feel Bullied by Others

Heavenly Father,
There are people in my life who reject me and break my heart.
I feel down and ashamed.
Give me the courage to withstand the hurtful words (and actions)
    of others.
No matter what persecutions I endure, help me to remember
    your great love for me.
Remind me that I am a beloved child of God.
You made me in your image.
With you, I am confident.
Help me to journey through each day peacefully, with purpose
    and joy.
Place your protective angels around me at all times.
Bless the person who is hurting me with your light to realize
    his/her wrong actions and to amend their ways.
Help each one of us to spread love and kindness in this world,
    to make it a better place for everyone.
In Jesus' name I pray. Amen.

A Prayer for When You Are Happy

My life is great today!
And I know, Lord,
that you are happy to see me happy.
To make life even better,
I will try to spread joy
all around me.
Amen.

A Prayer for When You Are Sad

Lord, I am sad.
I feel like crying.
Lord, why do we
have to be sad sometimes?
I want someone to help me feel better.
I feel like you're not even there.
But I know you don't want me to stay sad...
So help me laugh and be happy again.
Amen.

Thank You, Creator

I am thankful that the Creator
gave us a sun for warmth,
a moon to light the darkness,
food to fill our hunger,
families for comfort,
trees for air
and the stars in the sky
that will never stop
    shining.
Amen.

My Catholic Prayer Book
(Toronto: Novalis, 2017).

OCCASIONAL PRAYERS

Let's feel the love

Loving Jesus, we are often in awe when we look at the compassion and mercy that you demonstrated during your life on earth. You reached out to the downtrodden, the sinner, the loner, the leper, and the rejected. You did not judge these people; instead you showed your love and the love of your Father. Grant us the ability to reach out to all who are in need. May we refrain from judging, gossip, and criticizing others. Amen.

Help me find the way

Dear Lord, we often find it difficult to know what to choose and how to respond to many situations in our lives. Give us the discipline to acquire the knowledge we need to make good decisions. Grant us the ability and willingness to open our minds and hearts to the Holy Spirit as well as to follow the path upon which we are led. We also pray that we use the gift of prudence to discern between that which is constructive and that which is destructive. Amen.

Commitment is key

Dear God, help us to be committed to all those aspects of our lives that are in need of our attention and gifts. When we agree to be a part of some group, project, team or club, grant us the discipline and the wisdom we need to make our commitment real and meaningful. Keep us focused and on track so that we can reach our goals and feel good about the contributions we have made. Amen.

Dear God, help us to be committed to all those aspects of our lives that are in need of our attention and gifts. When we agree to be a part of some group, project, team or club, grant us the discipline and the wisdom we need to make our commitment real and meaningful. Keep us focused and on track so that we can reach our goals and feel good about the contributions we have made. Amen.

livingwithchrist.us

313

A YOUNG PERSON'S EXAMINATION OF CONSCIENCE

For use in preparing for the Sacrament of Reconciliation, based on The Ten Commandments

1. **God Comes First**
   - *Did I pray each day?*
   - *Did I act with respect in church?*
   - *Did I participate at Mass?*

2. **God's Name Is Holy**
   - *Did I always use God's name in the right way?*
   - *Did I treat and talk about holy things with respect?*

3. **God's Day Is Holy**
   - *Did I go to Mass on Sundays and Holy Days?*
   - *Did I miss Mass through my own fault?*

4. **Honor Mom & Dad**
   - *Did I obey my parents?*
   - *Did I treat them with respect?*
   - *Was I obedient and respectful to my teachers?*

5. **Do Not Kill**
   - *Have I been kind to my siblings and friends?*
   - *Did I hit or hurt anyone?*
   - *Did I harm anyone with mean or cruel words, whether in person or online?*

6. **Be Pure**
   - *Were my thoughts and actions good and pure?*
   - *Have I been careful to watch good movies and TV shows?*

7. **Do Not Steal**
   - *Have I always been honest?*
   - *Did I take anything that doesn't belong to me?*

8. **Do Not Lie**
   - *Have I always told the truth?*
   - *Have I spread rumors?*
   - *Have I been quiet about something when I should have spoken up?*

9. **Do Not Want Other People** and
10. **Do Not Want Their Things**
    - *Have I been satisfied with what I have?*
    - *Have I been jealous of another's things, toys or belongings?*
    - *Am I thankful for what I have?*

YEAR C AND THE GOSPEL OF LUKE

The Gospels of Matthew, Mark and Luke are known as the *synoptic* Gospels, a name which refers to the fact that these three books of the New Testament contain similar material, offering synopsis – or summary – of the life and ministry of Jesus.

Each year, the Gospel we hear on the majority of the Sundays in Ordinary Time that year rotates through these three books. This year (2024-2025) is what is known as Year C, the year which focuses on the Gospel of Luke.

The Gospel of Luke was written after the death of Jesus, likely around 80-100 AD, by the same person who wrote the Acts of the Apostles. It is the longest of the three synoptic gospels.

Among the best-known passages you will find in the Gospel of Luke are the story of the birth of Jesus, and the story of the disciples who meet the risen Jesus on the road to Emmaus.

The Gospel of Luke is famous for its parables, stories designed to teach a lesson to people. Among the parables you will find in the Gospel of Luke are those of the Good Samaritan, the Prodigal Son and the Lost Coin.

THE LITURGICAL YEAR

The readings for Sunday Mass and feast days change according to the liturgical calendar.

What is the liturgical year?
Throughout the year, Christians celebrate together important moments in Jesus' life. This is the liturgical year. There are five seasons: Advent, Christmas, Lent, Easter and Ordinary Time.

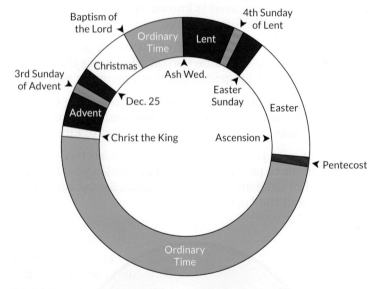

Advent is a time of waiting. It begins 4 weeks before Christmas. We prepare to welcome Jesus.

Christmas time celebrates the life of Jesus from his birth to his baptism. It includes Epiphany: Jesus welcomes the whole world.

During the 40 days of **Lent** we prepare for the great feast of Easter, the most important moment of the year.

Easter time is a season to celebrate Jesus' victory over death. It lasts from Easter Sunday to Pentecost, when the Holy Spirit comes upon the disciples.

The season in green above is called **Ordinary Time** because the Sundays are arranged using "ordinal numbers." It recounts many of the things Jesus did and said during his lifetime.

SACRAMENTS: A GIFT FROM GOD

Sacraments are rituals through which we receive God's grace. Grace is the gift of God's love and strength, given freely to us to help us lead good and just lives. Sacraments always involve signs appealing to our senses that point to God's saving presence in our lives. Baptism requires water, for example, and when we are confirmed, we are anointed with a special oil called chrism.

The seven sacraments of the Catholic Church are **Baptism, Reconciliation, Eucharist, Confirmation, Marriage, Holy Orders** and the **Anointing of the Sick**.

Sometimes you will hear people refer to **Sacraments of Initiation**, **Sacraments of Healing** and **Sacraments of Service**.

The **Sacraments of Initiation**—Baptism, Eucharist and Confirmation—help welcome us into a life of faith.

The **Sacraments of Healing** are Reconciliation and the Anointing of the Sick. Reconciliation helps us when our actions have injured our relationship with God, while the Anointing of the Sick helps us physically, mentally and spiritually when we face illness and suffering.

The **Sacraments of Service**—Marriage and Holy Orders (priesthood)—are linked to our call to serve others.

The sacraments of Baptism, Confirmation and Holy Orders can only be received once. As Catholics, we believe that when these sacraments are received, they leave a lasting mark—or seal—on the soul.

As Mass ends, the priest dismisses us with one of several prayers: "Go forth, the Mass is ended," for example, or "Go and announce the Gospel of the Lord." As people of faith, we are called to carry all that we have celebrated at Mass out into our daily lives.

There are several ways to do this:

- Prepare for Mass by reading the coming Sunday's first and second readings, the Psalm and the Gospel in advance, so that you are familiar with what you will hear at Mass. Try imagining yourself in the Gospel story, witnessing first-hand the story you will hear. Who might you be? What would your reaction be if you were to hear Jesus tell a parable? How would you feel if you were to witness Jesus perform a miracle? What must it have been like to travel with Jesus and listen to him teach and preach?

- After you have heard the Gospel proclaimed at Mass, ask yourself what message or idea really made an impression on you. Think about that throughout the week. If there is a phrase or passage that particularly appealed to you, try reciting it to yourself throughout the week. Think of ways it relates to you and to the world today.

- Listen closely to the priest's homily and ask yourself what you have learned from it. Reflect on that point throughout the week.

- Listen to the Prayer of the Faithful and remember who and what were being prayed for at Mass. Keep these petitions in mind as you say your prayers during the week. As you leave Mass, say to yourself, "This week I will pray for _____."

Guardian Angel Prayer

Angel of God, my guardian dear,
to whom God's love commits me here,
ever this day (night) be at my side,
to light and guard, to rule and guide. Amen.

Act of Contrition

My God,
I am sorry for my sins with all my heart.
In choosing to do wrong
and failing to do good,
I have sinned against you
whom I should love above all things.
I firmly intend, with your help,
to do penance,
to sin no more,
and to avoid whatever leads me to sin.
Our Savior Jesus Christ suffered and died for us.
In his name, my God, have mercy. Amen.

The Divine Praises

Blessed be God.
Blessed be his Holy Name.
Blessed be Jesus Christ, true God and true man.
Blessed be the Name of Jesus.
Blessed be his Most Sacred Heart.
Blessed be his Most Precious Blood.
Blessed be Jesus in the Most Holy Sacrament of the Altar.
Blessed be the Holy Spirit, the Paraclete.
Blessed be the great Mother of God, Mary most holy.
Blessed be her holy and Immaculate Conception.
Blessed be her glorious Assumption.
Blessed be the name of Mary, Virgin and Mother.
Blessed be St. Joseph, her most chaste spouse.
Blessed be God in his angels and in his Saints. Amen.

Grace Before Meals

Bless us, O Lord, and these, thy gifts
which we are about to receive
from thy bounty,
through Christ, our Lord,
Amen.

Grace After Meals

We give you thanks, Almighty God,
for all your benefits,
who lives and reign forever and ever.

May the souls of the faithful departed,
through the mercy of God,
rest in peace.
Amen.

Act of Faith

O my God, I firmly believe
that you are one God
in three divine persons,
Father, Son, and Holy Spirit.
I believe that your divine Son
became man and died for our sins,
and that he will come to judge
the living and the dead.
I believe these and all the truths
which the Holy catholic Church teaches,
because in revealing them
you can neither deceive nor be deceived.
Amen.